New Americans, New Promise

A Guide to the Refugee Journey in America

By Yorn Yan

FIELDSTONE
ALLIANCE

SAINT PAUL
MINNESOTA

Fieldstone Alliance is committed to strengthening the performance of the nonprofit sector. Through the synergy of its consulting, training, publishing, and research and demonstration projects, Fieldstone Alliance provides solutions to issues facing nonprofits, funders, and the communities they serve. Fieldstone Alliance was formerly Wilder Publishing and Wilder Consulting departments of the Amherst H. Wilder Foundation. If you would like more information about Fieldstone Alliance and our services, please contact Fieldstone Alliance, 60 Plato Boulevard East, Suite 150, Saint Paul, MN 55107, 651-556-4500.

We hope you find this book useful! For information about other Fieldstone Alliance publications, please see the ordering information on the last page or contact:

Fieldstone Alliance Publishing Center
60 Plato Boulevard East, Suite 150
Saint Paul, MN 55107

800-274-6024
www.FieldstoneAlliance.org

Edited by Vincent Hyman
Text designed by Kirsten Nielsen
Cover designed by Rebecca Andrews
Cover illustration by Kirsten Nielsen

First printing, October 2006
Manufactured in the United States

Library of Congress Data

Yan, Yorn, 1954-
  New Americans, new promise : a guide to the refugee journey in America / by Yorn Yan.
    p. cm.
  ISBN-13: 978-0-940069-50-3
  ISBN-10: 0-940069-50-4
  1. Refugees--United States. I. Title.
  HV640.4.U54Y36 2006
  362.870973--dc22
                          2006028636

About the Author

YORN YAN is a refugee from Cambodia. In 1979, he fled his home-land to the Thai-Cambodian border to avoid persecution and came to the United States in 1993. Yorn has devoted much of his life to improving the lives of refugees—first in refugee camps in Thailand and now in America. For eleven years, Yorn was a consultant with Wilder Center for Communities of the Amherst H. Wilder Foundation in Saint Paul, Minnesota. He is currently executive director of United Cambodian Association of Minnesota, a social service agency.

Yorn has been involved in many cross-cultural efforts, including the Bicultural Training Partnership, Southeast Asian Leadership Program, and the New-American Collaborative. In his work, he has met with refugees from Asia, Africa, Central America, Eastern Europe, and other parts of the globe. Yorn's work focuses on providing leadership, com-munity and organization development, management, program develop-ment, strategic planning, collaboration building, executive coaching, and training for nonprofit organizations and community groups. Yorn also serves on numerous nonprofit boards and government committees. He holds a bachelor's degree in human services and a master's degree in nonprofit management from Metropolitan State University.

Acknowledgments

First, I want to acknowledge my family members—my mother, who is my great leader; my wife and children, who support me in every way; and my brothers and sisters, who are always behind me in every step of my development. Thank you to my father and my youngest brother, who are always with me even though they are now gone from this world. Every one of them is special, and I cannot imagine doing this without their emotional and spiritual support.

Second, I want to share my deep gratitude to Beth Waterhouse and Vince Hyman for listening to my stories and especially for helping me with editing. Third, let me express my special thanks to refugee leaders, my former colleagues at the Wilder Foundation, my countless clients, and my "mainstream" friends for motivating me to write this book.

Next, I thank all those people who helped develop the content of this book. This includes all the focus group participants who shared their stories and thoughts with me—too many to name here. I would also like to thank the following people who took the time to review the final draft of this book and whose comments helped improve it: Emil Angelica, John Borden, Born Chea, Mark D. Franken, Sarah Gleason, Sheila Hoffman-Hick, Qamar Ibrahim, Barb Jeanetta, Yeshashw Kibour, Valerie Lee, Ellen Mercer, Joseph Moseray, Lisa Nguyen, Glenda Potter, and Sokhom Touch.

Finally, I would like to thank the David and Lucile Packard Foundation, which helped support this book.

Contents

Introduction

SOME 50,000 TO 90,000 REFUGEES and hundreds of thousands of others are resettled throughout the United States each year.[1] While the number of refugees and asylum seekers coming to the United States dropped dramatically after the events of September 11, 2001, the United States still accepts a large number of refugees from different parts of the world. As a result, our cities and rural areas are challenged to help these "New Americans" adjust to a new culture and language.

The United States is among the world's most generous refugee resettlement country.[2] Other generous refugee resettlement countries include Australia, Canada, Denmark, Finland, the Netherlands, New Zealand, Norway, Sweden, and Switzerland. Family reunification is the number one reason why most refugees and their families move to the United States. As soon as possible after a spouse or close relative has moved here and has become a U.S. citizen or lawful permanent resident, the family tries to get back together. This happens with the support of the U.S. immigration policy.

Many refugees come to the United States because of the threat of armed attack, countrywide violence, or mass killing. Some refugees have had a connection and relationship with the U.S. government in the past. Some fought side-by-side with Americans in their own countries against governments the United States opposed. Others supported

[1] Chapter 1 discusses some of the types of groups entering the United States.
[2] From Migration Information Source, www.migrationinformation.org.

an ideology of democracy or freedom that went against their dictatorial leaders' actions. Usually, the U.S. government (with the approval of Congress) agrees to provide these people with safety and protection and then brings some of them here.

Regardless of how and why they arrive, refugees face many challenges. They also pose challenges for the communities in which they settle. Many organizations that once served native-born Americans and communities now face the challenge of helping refugees—a challenge for which they are unprepared.

This book will help both refugees and the organizations that serve refugees in two ways. First, this book helps paint a picture of the developmental stages of refugees once they enter the United States. This approach is purposeful: the principle behind it is that you need to understand what the refugee experience feels like in order to understand how you can help refugees. Second, this book will help refugees help themselves by providing a general model of development against which they can gauge their own experiences and through which they can refine their aspirations.

Unlike many other books about refugees, this book is written by a person with an insider's knowledge of the refugee experience—a person who has dedicated his career to refugee issues.

My name is Yorn Yan. I was once a resident of Cambodia. Now I live in St. Paul, Minnesota, one of the "Twin Cities" of Minneapolis and St. Paul. Minnesota accepts many refugees and has the fortune of a richly diverse population. Many of these people are refugees and immigrants, like myself, and they come from around the globe—from Southeast Asia, from East and West Africa, from Central America, from Eastern Europe, and elsewhere. The arrival of refugees to Minnesota over the past three decades has invigorated the state and presented challenges similar to those faced by other refugee-welcoming states across the United States.

How This Book Was Written

This book grows out of the personal and professional experiences of the author. A refugee myself, I trained in a program meant to develop multicultural leaders. I then began working with other refugee groups as a consultant and executive director of a mutual assistance association (MAA). As I gained experience, I developed a model for refugee development. I tested this model with a variety of refugee individuals and groups and at several locations across the country. During the development of the model, I reviewed numerous publications. I worked with twelve focus groups consisting of seven to ten people each. The participants included both refugees (now American citizens) and native-born Americans who work professionally with refugee resettlement agencies. These individuals each had five to fifteen years of experience working with refugees. They represented various Asian, African, European, and Central American countries. I refined the model after discussions with these people. Next, a draft of the book was tested with various people and rewritten again in response to their comments. In all, three years of research, focus groups, and testing have gone into the development of this model. Much more will be learned as this book is circulated, but I have confidence that the basic model presented here will work for many people.

Who This Book Is For

This book is written to help many groups of people

- Native-born, fully acculturated Americans (sometimes called mainstreams), who work with refugees and immigrants. Such people are the program managers, staff, volunteers, and congregations of nonprofits, government agencies, religious institutions, and neighborhood and community groups that routinely interact with refugees.

- Neighborhood or community leaders and organizers, especially in rural and urban areas where refugees have settled or are beginning to settle.

- Consultants, technical assistance providers who serve groups that deal with refugees as a primary focus, or groups that are grappling with the challenges of serving refugees as a new client base.

- Decision makers—nonprofit executive directors and board members, government officials (city, county, state), legislators, corporate managers, and foundation representatives—who are deciding how to allocate resources around the challenge of helping refugees resettle.

- Refugee and immigrant leaders who are helping their own people prepare to move faster from one stage of development to another.

- School administrators and teachers who increasingly face the impact of refugee issues on their schools and communities.

This book is a primer, written for those of you who are beginning to grapple with the realities of refugee resettlement in your communities.

Longtime refugee experts will not find much new here, but I encourage you to use this work to help educate those who are new to refugee issues. And I hope that the five-stage model of refugee development is something that everyone can use to further the personal understanding of non-refugee populations and to reveal a pathway for refugees themselves.

How to Use This Book

By the end of this book, you will have a good understanding of how you and your organization can best assist refugees. To get to that point, you should understand the refugee experience and the five-stage model for how refugees can develop into successful members (and leaders) of American society. To that end, this book is organized to give you an overview of the refugee experience; to present in detail the refugee development model and advice for what refugees need at each stage; and, finally, to present suggestions for ways that your organization can work with refugee groups. Throughout, you'll find stories from refugees and from people who work with refugees and refugee groups. Here is what to expect in each chapter of the book:

Chapter 1 helps you understand the variety of refugees' experiences, issues, backgrounds, stories, and contributions. This chapter also provides different terms and definitions related to refugees.

Chapter 2 is an overview of the five stages of refugee development from the refugee's perspective—arriving, adjusting, climbing, achieving, and leading.

Chapters 3 through 7 describe each of the developmental stages in detail. Each chapter describes the refugee experience, typical challenges, and success factors. These chapters also suggest things refugees can do to help themselves at each stage and specific assistance refugee-serving organizations can provide.

Chapter 8 provides tools, advice, and guidance for those who serve refugees—such as government agencies, nonprofits, and corporations.

The Appendices cover three areas: Appendix A includes some resources that may be helpful to you; Appendix B includes general information on cross-cultural communication, especially how cultural differences influence conflict; and Appendix C summarizes the five developmental stages.

A warning

In preparing this book, I interviewed many refugees from many parts of the world. I tested the model with them, got their opinions and feedback, and modified the model and book accordingly. The goal is to help refugees understand some predictable stages of development that most will go through. Equally, the goal is to help the variety of people who encounter refugees better understand the challenges refugees face and the contributions they can make. THIS BOOK MAKES MANY GENERALIZATIONS. It has to, or else the book would be volumes and volumes long.

If you are a refugee reading this book, think about how and whether it applies to you. If you are a person who currently works with refugees or is planning to, remember that your first goal must always be to get to know each person and each group individually. The actual number of refugee development paths is equal to the actual number of refugees.

The actual number of refugee development paths is equal to the actual number of refugees...Respect each person and each group individually.

Every person is different. Every family is different. Every clan is different. Every culture is different. Respect each person and each group individually. Use the model for general understanding, preparation, and planning, but never assume that you know a person or a cultural group because of what you have read here. To do so is to miss the point of this book!

A Hope for Change

This book is written for native-born Americans, neighborhood and community leaders, consultants and technical assistance providers, refugee leaders and school administrators. The tools, tips, and advice provided in the book will help you to prepare yourself to work with different groups of refugees. Understanding their experiences, stages of development, and stories will increase your capacity and competence, so you will be able to effectively work with refugees.

My hope is that these stories, tips, tools, and practical advice will help you to be more creative when applying your current practices to refugee individuals and groups. Understanding the individual development of refugees (as a general process) will increase your capacity, knowledge, and skills when working with refugees, so you will spend fewer resources and get better results.

Chapter One

Understanding Refugees

SOME READERS OF THIS BOOK have long experience working with refugees. For them, this chapter will be review. But many foundations, nonprofit organizations, and agencies are just recognizing that they need to expand or change their services to help refugees; and corporations are hiring more and more refugees. This chapter will help non-refugees begin to understand the experience of refugees and the terms applied to them. But this chapter is not a substitute for your personal efforts to learn about refugees. Each refugee and each refugee group is different. To understand what they need, you must first take the time to develop a relationship with them. So, use this chapter to understand the basic refugee experience in a very general way. Think of this chapter as a way to help you understand the refugee experience from the outside in—stories and descriptions of the refugee experience. When we move to Chapters 2 through 6, you will begin to learn about the developmental stages of refugees as they adapt to life in the United States. Remember, that unless you, yourself, are a refugee, you will never fully understand the experience. But the developmental stages will help you begin to understand the refugee experience from the inside out.

Who Is a Refugee?

There are several definitions for refugee. The basic international-law definition of a refugee comes from the 1951 United Nations Convention Relating to the Status of Refugees. It defines a refugee as a person who is outside his or her county and is unable or unwilling to return to that country due to a well-founded fear that he or she will be persecuted because of race, religion, nationality, political opinion, or membership in a particular social group. This definition excludes persons displaced by national disasters or persons who, although displaced, have not crossed an international border. Also excluded are persons commonly known as "economic migrants," whose primary reason for flight has been a desire for personal betterment rather than persecution per se.

This 1951 UN Refugee Convention's agreement has served as the basis for defining refugees and their legal status. In order to deal with refugee problems around the world, the United Nations High Commissioner for Refugees (UNHCR) was established that same year to serve as the branch of the United Nations charged with the protection and assistance of refugees.[3] Persons defined as refugees under the UN Convention are entitled to the protection and status that it and its 1967 Protocol confer. UNHCR provides protection under these instruments and may also provide protection and assistance to other populations deemed to be "of concern" in refugee-like situations.

The 1951 United Nations Convention Relating to the Status of Refugees defines a refugee as a person from outside of the United States who seeks protection in this country on the grounds that he or she has a well-founded fear of persecution in his or her homeland as a result of race, religion, membership in a social group, political opinion, or national origin.[4]

The U.S. Refugee Act of 1980 (which amended the Immigration and Nationality Act) defines a refugee in words that closely track those of the UN Convention. This definition applies to the admission of persons as refugees to the United States under authorities conferred by the Act. The Act allows the President to extend this definition to certain persons still resident in countries he specifies.

---

[3] "Fact Sheet: Who Is a Refugee," released by the Bureau of Population, Refugees, and Migration, Department of State, Washington, DC: January 17, 1996.

[4] ibid.

GETTING TO KNOW A REFUGEE

If you are reading this book, you are probably already working with or beginning to encounter refugees. The following questions will help you better understand a refugee and what he or she needs in order to succeed.

1. What country did the individual consider home and what countries did he or she live in on the way here?

2. Why did the individual leave his or her homeland?

3. How long did the individual live in refugee camps before coming here?

4. How many family members are now living here?

5. How many family members are still in their home country (or scattered elsewhere)?

6. Who is his or her sponsor(s)?

7. How has the individual's sponsor(s) helped this family?

8. Is the individual a refugee or an immigrant? If you don't know, please find out.

9. Find out more about his or her background:
   — Religion?
   — Educational level?
   — Skills and work experiences?

10. How long has the person been in this country?

11. What is the individual's major barrier in this country?
    — Communicating in English?
    — Finding a job?
    — Physical or mental health issues?

12. What are the person's short-term needs (six months to a year)?

13. What is the person's main priority?
    — Learning English?
    — Getting a job?
    — Getting a driver's license?
    — Improving his or her job skills?
    — Understanding American culture?
    — Going to school?
    — Sending children to college?
    — Opening a business?
    — Getting to a leadership position?
    — Taking care of family members?
    — Other?

14. What was the person's dream before coming here?

15. What does the person want to be now and in the future?

16. What needs or support from outsiders will help this person achieve his or her goals?
    — Financial support?
    — Moral support?
    — Institutional support?
    — Guidance?
    — Other?

It is important to realize that people from other countries cannot simply decide to move to the United States. Generally, there are only two lawful ways to apply—as an immigrant or as a refugee. (Of course, some people find their own ways to enter into the United States illegally.)

Terms You Need to Know

There are distinct terms to define people who move from one place to another. These terms are defined by international laws and they include: refugee, immigrant, non-immigrant, asylum seeker, parolee, internally displaced person, exceptional leave to remain, or temporary protection.

Some of these terms have legal definitions and criteria attached to them—which bring both certain rights and certain restrictions—while others are in use but are less well defined. We'll first focus on the terms refugee and immigrant. Then we'll look at a number of other terms often heard in this work. Finally we'll explore the general psychic differences between refugees (and refugee-like people), who have fled or been forced to leave their country of birth, and immigrants, who have made a choice to leave their country of birth. This difference, in certain ways, is as important as the legal or technical distinctions.

You also can find these terms by going to International Thesaurus of Refugee Terminology at www.refugeethesaurus.org or to U.S. Department of Homeland Security, Citizenship, and Immigration Services' web site at www.uscis.gov/graphics/glossary.htm.

The information presented here is enough to get you started, but it is only an overview. The UN's web site, listed above, has scores of terms related to refugee work—far too much to cover in this introductory text.

Classifications of refugees [5]

The term *refugee* has come into common use to cover a range of people, including those displaced by natural disaster, poverty, or environmental

---

[5] Portions of this section are adapted from "USA for UNHCR," a web source at http://www. unrefugees.org/usaforunhcr/dynamic.cfm?ID=67, downloaded June 6, 2004.

pollution. For example, some people use the word economic refugees for those who leave their country or place of residence because they want to build a better life in a new place. The term refugee is often confused with immigrant, parolee, economic migrant, internally displaced person, exceptional leave to remain, temporary protection, and asylum seeker.

Before entering the United States, refugees are classified according to first, second, third, or fourth priority. You will need to understand these distinctions when you work with refugees who have settled in the United States. These processing priorities are defined by the Department of State's Bureau of Population, Refugees, and Migration. These priorities depend on the levels of danger, threat, or risk faced by refugees and the refugee's familial relationship to permanent residents or citizens of the United States.

To qualify for refugee resettlement in the United States, a person must come from a country designated by the Department of State as a refugee-sending country. The person must prove refugee status—a well-founded fear of persecution due to race, religion, membership in a social group, political opinion, or national origin. Refugees are classified into one of four priorities as follows:

First priority. Individuals are classified as first priority when they are in immediate danger of death and violence: for example, refugees whose camp is under attack, women at risk, victims of violence or torture, or those in urgent need of medical treatment. Also included are people who have no real chance of returning to their country of origin or becoming a part of the country to which they fled.

Second priority. Individuals are classified as second priority if they are from specific groups that are of concern to the United States. Hmong refugees in Thailand camps, for example, are included in this group.

Third priority. Individuals classified as third priority are the relatives (spouses, parents, and unmarried children) of United States permanent resident aliens, refugees, asylum seekers, conditional residents, or parolees. Also included are the unmarried children under the age of twenty-one of U.S. citizens and the parents of citizens who are under twenty-one.

Fourth priority. Fourth priority is granted to the married children, siblings, grandparents, or other more distant relatives of United States permanent resident aliens, refugees, asylum seekers, conditional residents, or parolees.

For each region or country, the Department of State Bureau of Population, Refugees, and Migration decides which priorities will be considered. Not all priorities are considered for all countries.

Figure 1, U.S. Refugee Selection and Admission Process, provides an overview.

Legal immigrants

An immigrant is a person who leaves one country to settle permanently in another. There are at least three ways in which people called immigrants can legally enter the United States. These three groups of immigrants are: 1) family-sponsored immigrants, 2) employment-based immigrants, and 3) those who win a diversity lottery. We'll look at each of these three kinds of immigrants.

1. *Family-sponsored immigrants.* The United States government offers up to 480,000 visas per year to the immediate families of U.S. citizens and legal residents who are willing to sponsor family members and who have the financial ability to support them. This group of people might come from a refugee camp or their country of origin.

2. *Employment-based immigrants.* Each year the U.S. government offers 140,000 visas to employers to bring in skilled workers. These kinds of workers include professors, researchers, or skilled workers in high-demand fields. The number can be changed based on the need for skilled employees from abroad.

3. *Diversity lottery.* The United States accepts up to 55,000 visas per year for those who win a diversity lottery. This lottery allocates immigrants to countries that are under-represented in other forms of U.S. immigration. Applicants must be age eighteen or older with the equivalent of a high school diploma.

FIGURE 1. U.S. REFUGEES SELECTION AND ADMISSION PROCESS

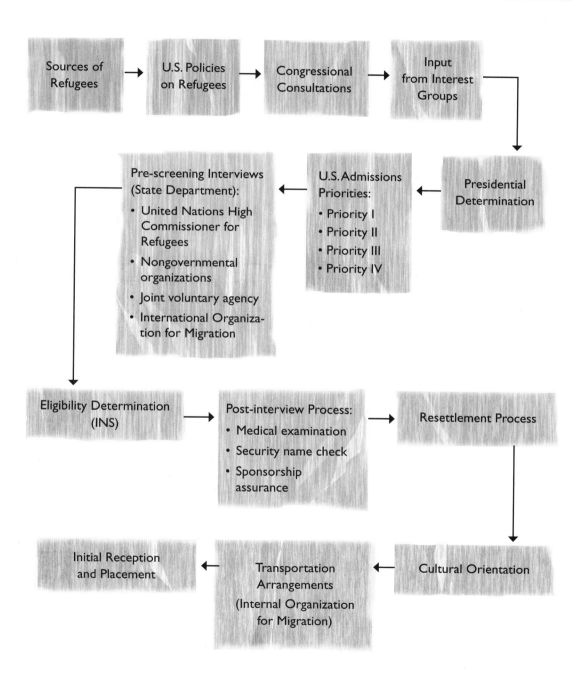

Naturalized citizen

Lawful Permanent Residents can apply for U.S. citizenship through the process of naturalization. To qualify, an applicant must have resided in the United States for at least five years (three years if married to a U.S. citizen), demonstrate a basic knowledge of U.S. history and government, have committed no serious crimes, have paid their U.S. taxes, be of "good moral character," and demonstrate that they can understand, speak, and write ordinary English.

Other terms

There are many ways of classifying people who enter (or may soon enter) the United States, as well as some other important terms you'll run into, as follows:

Non-immigrant: A non-immigrant is an individual who is permitted to enter the United States for a period of limited duration and for a limited purpose. Non-immigrant visas may be issued to students, tourists, temporary workers, business executives, diplomats, and others who will be returning to their home country after a defined period.

Asylum seeker: An asylum seeker is a person who has left his or her country of origin because she or he fears persecution if sent back to his or her homeland. This individual has already entered the United States, so she or he may apply for asylum here on the same grounds as a refugee.

Parolee: A parolee is a person who has been allowed to enter the United States for humanitarian reasons for a prescribed time—she or he may not necessarily live here permanently.

Undocumented immigrant: An undocumented immigrant is any immigrant who is in the United States without the permission of the U.S. government. Undocumented immigrants typically enter the United States either illegally, without being inspected by a U.S. immigration officer or by using false document, or legally, with a temporary visa, but remains in the United States beyond the expiration date of the visa.

Mainstreams: A mainstream is a native-born American of any background—people who have grown up in American society and understand it from the inside out. From a refugee perspective, all native-born Americans are "mainstreams." (In this book, we use the term native-born American; however, in some parts of the country, the term "mainstreams" is used to refer to the native-born Americans.)

New arrival: A refugee who has been in the final resettlement country for a relatively short time, perhaps one to three years.

New American: A refugee who has been in the United States for perhaps five years or more, who understands American systems and culture, and who may have acquired citizenship status. Some people whose history includes being a refugee prefer to be called "New Americans" because they feel that there is a stigma attached to the term refugee. They feel the term New American represents their efforts to become part of American society. Also, the term helps the individual assemble a new identity—to cease thinking of him- or herself as someone who is seeking refuge but as someone who is making a new home and life.

A FEW TERMS USED OUTSIDE THE UNITED STATES

Exceptional Leave to Remain (ELR). This term refers to groups of people uprooted by civil war, who fall outside the UN definition of refugees because they have not been individually targeted for persecution. Asylum seekers who do not meet the criteria of the 1951 UN Convention but nevertheless need protection may be granted ELR status.

Internally Displaced Person (IDP). An internally displaced person may have been forced to flee his or her home for the same reasons as a refugee, but has not crossed an internationally recognized border. There are more IDPs in the world than refugees.

Temporary Protection. When a large group of people seek asylum from a particular country because of persecution or upheaval, determination of refugee status may be temporarily suspended and temporary protection granted. For example, individual Kosovo Albanians were granted temporary protection in 1999, as were Bosnian Muslims during the Bosnian conflict from 1992 to 1995.

Mind first or body first?

People born in the United States often cannot differentiate between the concept of refugee and that of immigrant. After all, both come from a foreign land to make a new home in the United States—so how could they differ? But there are very important distinctions. Two words— mind and body—are at the crux of the distinction. Immigrants come to the United States with their mind first and their body later. That is, they make plans to leave their country of origin and look forward to creating a new life in a new land. Their vision is an active, positive one, led by their mental picture of a future that they control. So, they leave their home with their mind first, and willingly bring their body along for the ride.

There's an important psychic difference between immigrants and refugees once they have arrived in their new country. *Immigrants* have made a choice to pursue a future in a new land. *Refugees* have fled a life-threatening situation. Immigrants arrive in America mind first, followed by body: a dream fulfilled. Refugees arrive body first and later adjust their vision to fit their new reality.

In contrast, refugees come to the United States with their body first. Only later does their mind adapt to the change. Remember, refugees flee their home country in fear and then seek refugee status in a country of asylum. The process of getting to the United States often takes years, involves many steps, and is usually not an "option" but their only hope for a safe life. Their mental image is of a home lost and of an uncertain future—a future that is not of their own choice or creation. They are reacting to human and environmental catastrophe. They carry with them the vision of a type of life that was taken from them rather than a vital new future that they chose. Eventually, most refugees adapt and accept the new situation, and begin to develop a vision for what they may make of their life in their new land. So, they arrive first in body, and much later in mind.

As with all things human, there is tremendous difference from one person to the next, even given the exact same circumstances. But in general, the "mind first or body first" analogy should help native-born Americans understand the psychic differences between refugees and immigrants. For more about the legal differences between refugees and immigrants in the United States, see Immigration and Nationality Act, Section 101(a) (42). There may also be confusion about the difference between refugee and asylum seeker. The criteria for determining a person's status as asylum seeker are the same as for refugee status.

The only difference is in where the application takes place. Refugee application occurs before a person enters the United States. Asylum requests come from people who are already in the United States. International law recognizes the right to seek asylum but does not obligate states to provide it.

The Refugee Experience

Refugees enter the United States from Central America, Southeast Asia, Eastern Europe, East and West Africa, the Middle East, and elsewhere. They leave their own countries to escape war, violence, persecution, and imprisonment. There is often little choice for some refugees, who can either flee their countries or be killed or persecuted. They do not waste time—they just pick up their children and run for their lives.

Because refugees leave their countries with no time for preparation, they leave behind almost everything: family records, professional documents, diplomas, photographs, and other valuable items. Far worse, they often leave behind family members such as a spouse, children, parents, and relatives.

People leave their country because of civil wars, wars between two countries, wars within a region, persecution, imprisonment, and starvation. Many refugees are victims of torture or they directly witness violence and killing. They have an inerasable experience of ruthless behavior and tyrannical power of their former leaders. They are in constant fear of the authorities, and they don't trust people other than family members and close friends. Refugees are people without homes or destinations, but their hope for a better life is always with them. Some of them have a dream to go back to their homeland when situations get better.

To paint a general picture, most refugees follow this path:

- They escape persecution—including violence, harassment, and killing—in their own country.

- They flee to a refugee camp of some sort. They may try to return home, come back to the refugee camp, or move to another refugee camp one or more times. Eventually, they receive permission to settle in the United States.

- They settle in the United States and begin adapting to a new culture and a new language.

UNHCR refers only about 1 percent of all refugees for resettlement in a third country. Only refugees who have been referred by UNHCR or by the U.S. embassy in the country of asylum are eligible for the U.S. Refugee Resettlement Program. Fewer than 80,000 refugees participated in U.S. Refugee Resettlement Programs in 2005.[6] Thus, those who arrive in the United States are carefully selected. The government decides which refugees are allowed to enter, based on its priorities.

The refugee journey

While each refugee's personal experience is different, all refugees had no choice but to leave their country or face violence, persecution, or death. Escaping is the most dangerous, frightening experience that most refugees go through, and not all of them make it. Some are captured and put in prison by their own government, their own people, while others lose limbs, friends, spouses, or family members to land mines or thugs.

I have listened to many stories of how refugees escape from their countries to safe places. While no two stories are alike, certain themes emerge from the stories of refugees, whether from Asia, Africa, or other parts of the world:

- Fighting occurs between two armed groups in the middle of a town of thousands of people; shells hit some homes.

- Family members decide that it is too dangerous to stay, so they leave their home with some belongings.

- Family members travel by foot for miles from one place to another in order to find a new safe place to stay temporarily.

---

[6] "How Refugees Come to America," http://www.refugeesusa.org/article.aspx?id=1082&subm=40&ssm=47&area=Investigate.

- They reach a town or village where some of their relatives live, and they stay there for a couple of months hoping to return home.

- Fighting spreads, coming closer and closer to that place, and the family, along with thousands of others, move again to the border of a neighboring country.

- While escaping, some family members are killed; the elderly cannot walk and must be carried or left behind to die; children cry for food and water; others are sick; a few wounded people are left behind; some children do not have parents with them; and everybody is exhausted, frustrated, and hopeless.

- At the border of the two countries they see signs of Red Cross or UNHCR (United Nations High Commissioner for Refugees). They receive food, water, medicine, and plastic tarps for shelter.

- Thousands of people stay in a temporary place for months. One night, fighting erupts again near the camp and family members run for their lives. As a result, some families are split up—perhaps permanently.

- This large group of people moves deeper inside of a neighboring country and is allowed to stay there—usually in an UNHCR refugee camp because the host country has allowed UNHCR to set up camps for the refugees.

In this story of flight, rest, and flight again, terror and suffering are the norm. Refugees lose family members to killings, mines, starvation, or other unnatural disasters. Some witness the murder of their family members. Some young refugees flee without parents, become separated during flight, or see them die during escape. Nearly all refugees lose their social and political status.

Take a moment to put yourself in this place. You flee with your family. In a crush of people, you and your children are separated from your spouse. You and your children walk for days, wondering how you will care for your children alone. Then imagine that your children watch as you yourself fall. Imagine the risks facing your children completing the journey to a refugee camp and then living there without parents.

ONE FAMILY'S STORY

On April 17th, 1975, a communist guerrilla group called Khmer Rouge, led by Pol Pot, took power in Phnom Penh, the capital of Cambodia. Approximately 2 million Cambodians died by starvation, torture, or execution. In 1979, the Vietnamese invaded and liberated the Cambodian people from Khmer Rouge. Many Cambodians saw no difference between the Khmer Rouge and the grim new regime installed by Vietnam. Like the Khmer Rouge, it offered no rights or freedoms. These people faced a difficult choice and asked themselves thousands of times, "Do we seek freedom or death?" Some 600,000 fled to camps along the border of Thailand.

Among these people was a family of four brothers, two sisters, and a mother. In 1979, they crossed the Thai-Cambodian border and entered a refugee camp in Thailand, hoping to find a safer life. One night, in 1985, a fight broke out in the camp between Vietnamese troops and anti-communist movement fighters called the Khmer People National Liberation Front (KPNLF). During this fight, three of the brothers were separated from their sisters, mother, and eldest brother, and joined hundreds of thousand Cambodians who were forced to move deeper inside the border of Thailand. There, the brothers were welcomed by United Nations' staff in a refugee camp called Khao I Dang Camp. In time, they received their refugee status. Meanwhile, their oldest brother, two sisters, and mother all stayed in a refugee camp located along the border. Two years later, the two sisters and mother decided to cross the border into Khao I Dang Camp in order to find a safer place to live and to join the three brothers. Their reunion was joyful, but these three family members, who had just entered into the camp, were not qualified for refugee status. Because they were not registered, they did not get food or water from the United Nations for months. Without United Nations identification cards, they had to avoid Thai authorities, hiding like rats underground. After six months, Thai authorities searched for and captured the two sisters and their mother and transported them back to a refugee camp along the border called Site Two Camp. Seven years later, the three brothers became American citizens and sponsored their brother, sisters, and mother to come the United States.

That family is, in fact, my family. Sadly, my father and youngest brother were not with us in the camps or later in America. They were among those who died in Cambodia. Our story is just one of thousands. I have heard this kind of story almost everywhere. Lack of food and security are common problems faced by refugees while in the protection of the UN and in the authority of the second country. There are no safe places at night in refugee camps. Refugees experience or hear shootings in the camps by armed people demanding money or forcing children to join the armed forces. Refugees experience life as the lowest class people. It is miserable.

—Yorn Yan

Life in refugee camps

In refugee camps or in first countries of asylum, international organizations play very important roles in assisting refugees. These agencies include the United Nations High Commissioner for Refugees (UN-HCR), the International Committee of the Red Cross, the International Organization for Migration (IMO), and the U.S. Committee for Refugees and Immigrants. They provide food, shelter, protection, other basic needs, transportation, and screening processes for refugees.

Lack of nutrition, security, and safety in the camps are common problems that refugees face. Most of them do not have enough food to eat or even water to drink. The United Nations' programs offer nutrition to the refugees, but only enough to survive. Refugees who lack identification cards or are not on the correct registration list may not have food for months because they do not qualify for UN programs. They have to depend on family members or friends to survive. Food and water are limited for each member of a family. What happens when more family members arrive or children are born?

Even in refugee camps where United Nations staff or authorities of the second country offer protection, refugees are not safe. United Nations or UNHCR programs protect refugees during the day, but not at night. Some women are raped while they escape or while they stay in the refugee camps. Children are recruited or forced to join the army. Their rights are violated. Refugees feel as though they have no rights or freedom, so their lives come down to hopelessness about unsecured and uncertain futures.

Some refugees stay in a camp for five or ten years. Year after year, no countries will take them or they have no family to sponsor them. They dream that one day they will cross an ocean and live in a new land. They imagine reuniting with family members from whom they have been separated for decades. Although some refugees die in refugee camps without reaching their dream destination or fulfilling their goals, they hope that their children will have bright futures and better lives.

How Does It Feel?

Imagine this.

You've lived all your life at peace.

Home, family, friends, all normal.

Then, without warning, your whole world changes.

Overnight, lifelong neighbors become enemies. Tanks prowl the street and buses burn. Motor shells shatter the mosques. Rockets silence the church bells.

Suddenly everything you've known and owned and loved is gone and, if you're lucky enough to survive, you find yourself alone and bewildered in a foreign land. You are a refugee.

Source: United Nations High Commissioner for Refugees

Each morning, refugees arise and reawaken hope for themselves and their family members. Refugees are at the same time hopeless and hopeful people. They are hopeless because they cannot do things they want to do while they stay in the refugee camp. They have lost everything they own. They have no place to live and nowhere to go. They do not know what their future looks like. Yet they are also hopeful people. They believe that bad things will end some day and good things will come in the near future. They hold onto their dream of having a safer place to live.

Most refugees do not have a plan to come to the United States or any specific country. Nor do they know how to prepare for a new life in a new country. They have no idea what other countries look like, but returning to their home country is not an option for most refugees. So, they decide they must find a new country for their safety and their children's future. They fill out application forms with the assistance of the United Nations staff and send them to as many countries as they can. Eventually, they are accepted and fly to their new home.

Life in the new country

In the United States there are national and local agencies, churches, and volunteer organizations assisting refugees in their resettlement. Some examples of these organizations include Church World Service (CWS), Episcopal Migration Ministries (EMM), Ethiopian Community Development Council (ECDC), Hebrew Immigrant Aid Society (HIAS), Iowa Department of Human Services, International Rescue Committee (IRC), the U.S. Committee for Refugees and Immigrants (USCRI), United States Conference of Catholic Bishops (USCCB), and World Relief Refugee Services (WRRS). At the community level there are mutual assistance associations (MAAs), which are refugee-run organizations.

The U.S. Department of State's Bureau of Population, Refugees, and Migration (PRM) provides funds to the International Organizations for Migration and various U.S. volunteer agencies to support their work in the areas of refugee processing, overseeing cultural orientation, transportation, and reception and placement services in the United States. The Department of Health and Human Services (DHHS) Office of Refugee Resettlement (ORR) provides funds and coordinates domestic refugee assistance programs.

People from the same region generally tend to concentrate in certain areas of the United States. This occurs because newcomers like to live close together or enter preexisting, welcoming communities. Also, some states have resettlement agencies or communities that are more welcoming than others. For example, many Vietnamese and Iranians settle in California and more Cubans settle in Florida than all states combined. Many refugees from the Soviet Union, Sierra Leone, and Liberia live in New York; Hmong, Somali, and Ethiopian refugees live in Minnesota; and a large number of Sudanese live in Texas.

At least five factors come into play when refugees choose where to live:[7]

• Family or friends are in the area

---

[7] These five factors were uncovered during interviews and focus groups with refugees. In addition, these factors are supported by research done by the Wilder Research Center. See the article, "Speaking for Themselves: A Survey of Hispanic, Hmong, Russian, and Somali Immigrants in Minneapolis-Saint Paul" by Paul Mattessich and Ginger Hope, a Wilder Research Center report for the St. Paul Pioneer Press (Nov. 2000): 7–8. http://www.wilder.org/research/reports.html?summary=89.

- Jobs are easy to find
- Good schools exist for their children
- Services are available when they need help
- People are welcoming

This does not mean that all refugees pre-select where to live within the United States. Refugees typically move from one place to another until they find the best place for them and their families. Affordable housing and personal security also influence the choice of community in which to settle.

Refugees' first experiences in the United States

Once in the United States, refugees spend many years adjusting to American cultural norms, learning English, building new careers, and creating new lives. According to the United Nations' report, a great percentage of refugees entering the United States are victims of torture,[8] and they need special treatment beyond standard health care services. Along the way, many refugees experience racism, discrimination, and unfair treatment by others.

Commonly, the elderly population and children have challenges due to malnutrition and lack of medicine. Some suffer depression, perhaps stemming from lack of safety and social isolation because of their long stay in refugee camps.

Adult refugees with families focus their goals, hopes, and dreams more on their children than on themselves. They hope that their children will have better and brighter futures. They anticipate that their children will pursue higher educations. They hope that their children become productive citizens and have few troubles in their lives. Refugees hope that their children's generation will keep up the language and culture of their origin, even as they learn a new language and culture. For example, refugees often note cultural values and customs that they want to see preserved, such as respect for elders, parents, and the family.

Refugee families usually hope to become U.S. citizens and plan to stay in America as their permanent home. They hope to live close to their

[8] U.S. Refugee Admissions Program Report in 2002.

family members. Some parents want their children to stay with them after they finish high school or college. Although many have plans to visit their homelands on a regular basis, few consider permanent relocation to their country of origin.

Many refugees come from areas where males and females have very different roles and men have more power than women. Once in the United States, many refugees want to see women become more equal

CRITICAL ROLES OF U.S. RESETTLEMENT AGENCIES

U.S. resettlement agencies have played critical roles in assisting refugees. These agencies sponsor refugees and their families into the United States, find homes and shelters for refugees when they first arrive, provide services that meet immediate needs, and help search for jobs. Some of these agencies have assisted states, counties, voluntary agencies, refugee-led organizations, social service providers, employers, and policy makers in helping refugees achieve self-sufficiency.

Many states provide funding to local agencies to assist refugees with immediate and long-term needs. The state programs are funded through the Office of Refugee Resettlement and coordinate their work local providers of resettlement services.

For more information about refugees and programs helping refugees you can go to the following U.S. resettlement agencies' web sites.

Church World Service at www.churchworldservice.org

Ethiopian Community Development Council at www.ecdcinternational.org

Episcopal Migration Ministries at www.dfms.org

Hebrew Immigrant Aid Society at www.hias.org

Iowa Department of Human Services at www.dhs.state.ia.us

International Rescue Committee at www.theirc.org

Lutheran Immigration and Refugee Service at www.lirs.org

U.S. Committee for Refugees and Immigrants at www.refugees.org

United States Conference of Catholic Bishops at www.nccbuscc.org

to men both inside a marriage and outside the home. Some men, however, are not ready to accept these changes, which leads to marital conflict between husband and wife. Meanwhile, family members want to see an end to divorce and domestic violence. But the different U.S. culture often increases pressures that lead to family strife.

Refugees and their families enjoy the freedoms and opportunities they have in the United States. One opportunity that a refugee waits for is to become a U.S. citizen, and refugees grasp this opportunity when it comes. Citizenship helps refugees feel more secure. As U.S. citizens, they can do whatever they want to do as long as they follow the laws

REFUGEE-RUN ORGANIZATIONS LEAD THE WAY

Refugees who lead mutual assistance associations help refugees adjust to life in the United States, advocate for other refugees, and build bridges between refugees and mainstream American communities. Most of these organizations provide direct services to their community members, particularly serving their own ethnic or cultural communities within a small geographic area. Some refugee-run organizations extend their services to groups of refugees other than their own by using their experience as refugees.

The number of refugee-run organizations is increasing due to the increase of the number of experienced refugee leaders. Most of these refugee-run organizations receive funds from the government (federal, state, or county), from private foundations, and from their community members. They want to help their own people to get out of poverty or to build better lives in the new society. However, many of these organizations are not run effectively and only a small number survive.

Refugee-run organizations play important roles in helping first-generation refugees build new lives in the new society—but beyond that, they also help the children of refugees better understand their parents' cultures as well as American culture. Some refugee-run organizations work in partnership with mainstream social service providers or large institutions to help address the needs and issues faced by their refugee community. Refugee-run organization leaders realize that they can't help their own community without outside assistance because problems are complex and difficult to resolve, and some issues, such as mental health, are beyond the organization's capacity.

of the country, bringing an increased sense of power and choice. Even though they become U.S. citizens, some refugees go back to visit in their home countries to open businesses; to work with international agencies in addressing social, economic, or political issues; or to stay there after their retirement as their country of birth becomes more secure.

Complex Issues, Remarkable Contributions

Refugees face tremendous difficulties in their lives—first, when forced to flee their homes, then in refugee camps, and finally in the United States. Some issues, such as depression, are long term and often hard for others to understand. These issues are too complex to be solved without help. Sometimes the refugees do not want to discuss their problems with others or they do not know how to describe their problems to others. Some of these issues occur before the refugee comes to the United States, while others occur as part of resettlement in the United States.[9] Chapter 3 describes these issues in detail, but following is an overview of the issues.

As noted, before coming to the United States, refugees live in fear and suffer for years. From loss of safety, loss of identity, health, property, and family, they face countless problems in their lives. Women raise children without the help of spouses or extended family; sometimes children raise other children. Physical violence, sexual violence, mistreatment, and terror are common.

Refugees arrive in the United States with many skills that suited their former lives, but with little if any preparation for what life is like in the United States. Some refugees develop physical and mental health problems such as post-traumatic stress disorder, deep grief from loss of home and loved ones, distrust of government. Once in their new country, refugees face new issues such as finding jobs, finding affordable housing, finding appropriate day care for their children, or learning transportation systems. Some refugees don't speak English well

---

[9] Colleagues have pointed out that refugees face similar problems regardless of where they resettle. However, the focus of this book is on refugees in the U.S.

and lack formal education. Many don't know American culture. They must learn new ways to balance work, home, and school. Some may not have the time to fully focus on their resettlement.

A few refugees get "lost" and never find their way back. America is too big, too complex, and too modern, with too many laws and too many choices! These lost refugees can't connect the dots of their lives, from escaping violence to living in refugee camps to new and confusing lives in the United States. Some refugees miss everything they leave behind: their families, their homes, properties, climate, religious practices, and so much more. Some refugee adults and elderly want to return as soon as situations in their home countries improve, but very soon their children acculturate. Once the second generation becomes "American" they want to remain. A generational rift ensues, adding to the refugee's psychic pain. As children attend school in the United States, the tensions grow deeper. Family problems among refugees have become an issue that many social service agencies are trying to address.

Remember that refugees are skilled survivors. Many faced conditions and experiences that native-born Americans simply can't imagine. The capacity of most refugees to overcome challenges and barriers is extraordinary. This strength is what helps refugees make so many contributions to America.

To help the people who get lost, we must understand their real problems. Of course, we understand their problems better when they can explain them to us. Unfortunately, some refugees cannot fully identify their own problems or why they feel lost. Sometimes these people are adults and elders who have had horrific, life-changing experiences and truly may face challenges for the rest of their life.

But remember that refugees are skilled survivors. Many faced conditions and experiences that native-born Americans simply can't imagine. The capacity of most refugees to overcome challenges and barriers is extraordinary. It is something to be honored and respected, and a remarkable asset that refugees can call on again and again. This strength is what helps refugees make so many contributions to America.

There are some people who think that refugees are a burden on the United States—that refugees do not pay taxes or that Americans have to take care of them. If you are reading this book, you probably are not among those who hold this mistaken notion. Still, it's important to review the major contributions refugees make to American culture, business, and democracy—so you can share the reality with your colleagues who have not had the good fortune of observing refugee contributions and may need to have their eyes opened.

It is difficult to find research in the United States that focuses specifically on the impact of refugees, but many people have researched the economic consequences of immigration. The Greater Twin Cities United Way conducted research in 2002 on the topic. Among their findings: "The level of employment growth that is created by recent immigrants from other countries is equal to or greater than that of the growth created by the relocation of domestic U.S. residents within the United States. This includes both job creation as well as consumed goods and services."[10]

As members of the U.S. workforce and as taxpayers, refugees help build American society and the economy. Many fill low-paying jobs in hotels, nursing homes, parking lots, restaurants, or construction. Some refugees are well educated and arrive prepared with technical skills. Most bring the willingness to work hard to build their lives, and thus the American economy. Some refugees are business owners, investors, students, teachers, doctors, and consumers. Per one study, "Overall…the impact of immigration on the economy…may run on the order of $1 to $10 billion a year. This gain may be modest relative to the size of the United States' economy, but it remains a significant positive gain in absolute terms."[11]

Research in the United Kingdom has explored refugees' contributions there. According to "The Heritage and Contribution of Refugees in the UK: A Credit to the Nation," "Our refugee communities have also helped to shape the British cultural landscape, generating artists, musicians, sport-people, chefs, and innovative thinkers, and making Britain one of the most diverse and richly multicultural societies in Europe today." The authors add, "Far from being a drain on Britain's finances,

---

[10] Karen Meade, MSc, "Immigrants and the Economy" (Saint Paul, MN: Greater Twin Cities United Way Research and Planning Department, 2002), 2.

[11] J.P. Smith and B. Edmonston, *The New Americans: Economic, Demographic, and Fiscal Effects of Immigration* (Washington, DC: National Academy Press, 1997), 53, as cited in Meade on page 2.

over the years refugees have had a positive economic impact, bringing new skills and ideas into the country and putting the resourcefulness and determination that drove them to seek asylum to use in British workplaces."[12]

Summary

This first chapter has been one of definition and direction. You've learned that refugees have lived amazing and stressful lives prior to arriving in the United States. The issues they face after arriving in the United States are no less complex, and yet most refugees go on to become active contributors to the communities in which they settle. Finally, you've learned some important definitions, including the difference between a refugee and an immigrant. The background in this chapter sets the stage for the five stages of refugee development described in Chapter 2 and detailed in Chapters 3 through 7. It will also prepare you to plan the work of your agency, as discussed in Chapter 8.

---

[12] Research in the UK has shown that refugees are a net contributor to the economy; it is logical to generalize that outcome to the United States. "The Heritage and Contribution of Refugees in the UK-A Credit to the Nation," page 10. White paper, http://www.refugeeweek.org.uk/NR/rdonlyres/F90B58C1-0879-4EF1-BA95-4C8D082B084F/0/HistoryofContributions.pdf.

ECONOMIC CONTRIBUTIONS

While data specific to refugee contributions is rare, much work has been done to uncover the economic impact of immigrants. The following facts may help as you make support case for refugees in your community.

- An immigrant and his or her children will pay on average about $80,000 more in taxes during their lifetimes than they collect in government services.

- Immigrants with college degrees will pay $198,000 more in taxes during their lifetime than they collect in government services.

- In 1997, the United States reaped a $50 billion surplus from taxes paid by immigrants to all levels of government.

- Without the contribution of immigrant labor, the output of goods and services in the United States would be at least $1 trillion smaller than it is today.

- The total net benefit (taxes paid less benefits received) to the Social Security system if current levels of immigration remain constant is nearly $500 billion for the 1998–2022 period and nearly $2 trillion through 2072.

- Immigrants collectively earn $240 billion a year, pay $90 billion a year in taxes, and receive $5 billion in welfare.

- Immigrants who become U.S. citizens typically pay more in taxes than native-born Americans. Federal taxes paid by families with a naturalized citizen average $6,580 per year compared with $5,070 for native-born-only families.

- Businesses founded by immigrants are a source of substantial economic and fiscal gain for U.S. citizens.

- The average immigrant contributes about $25,000 to local and state governments.

From "Quick Facts on Immigrant Contributions to the United States Economy," People for the American Way, www.pfaw.org/pfaw/general/default.aspx?oid=14332.

Chapter Two

Five Stages of Refugee Development

CHAPTER 2 PROVIDES AN OVERVIEW of the five developmental stages of refugees.[13] These stages were observed and developed relative to the refugee experience. As discussed earlier, these stages were not developed with regard to immigrants, who may have motives and goals that differ from refugees.

Always keep in mind that this model of refugee development is just a model. It is not a fact. You need to get to know each refugee individually to understand in what ways your agency can be of service.

As you have read in the first chapter, refugees are forced to leave their home countries to escape wars, violence, or persecution. Their lives or lives of their family members are in danger. They come here with their body first. They do not prepare to come here like immigrants do. But that does not mean that the refugee people do not want to improve their lives or find better jobs here. Actually, as you will see

---

[13] The five stages described in this book are based on my personal experience and my discussions with other refugees from various countries of origin. Some authors have described various adjustment phases during resettlement efforts, and some colleagues who reviewed drafts of this book noted similarities in models of immigrant adjustment. For another model of refugee development, see Chapter 3 of the online publication "New Neighbors, Hidden Scars" by the Center for Victims of Torture, www.cvt.org/new_neighbors/New_Neighbors_Hidden_Scars_chap_3a.pdf.

in the five developmental stages, refugees work hard to improve their situations and take leadership roles in society. The five developmental stages are:

Stage 1: Arriving

Stage 2: Adjusting

Stage 3: Climbing

Stage 4: Achieving

Stage 5: Leading

Figure 2, The Five Stages of Refugee Development, presents a picture of the process.

The stages are presented as an upward progression, and overall, they are. However, a person does not travel straight from stage one to stage two in these five developmental stages, but spirals among the stages or travels up and down several times.

Passing from one stage to another is not simple and requires both internal and external support. Internal supporters are sponsors, family members, and close friends. External supporters are coworkers, social service providers, community groups, and social systems. Most refugees and refugee-sponsored family members go through the first and second stages. Most reach the third stage and remain there, but fewer move to the fourth. In fact, the last two stages may not apply for most refugees; for those who bring children or have them in the United States, these latter stages may be embodied in their children. Still, the model itself can be an inspiration for refugees whether they have just arrived or been in the United States for decades.

It is easy to look at a chart like this and think that because one stage has a higher number than another, a person in that stage is "better" than a person at a lower stage. The stages are meant to represent only the level of success of the individual as they adapt to American society.

Figure 2. The Five Stages of Refugee Development

The pyramid shape of Figure 2 reflects both the refugee's upward mobility when moving through the stages and the number of refugees who move into these stages—that is, the higher up the pyramid, the fewer refugees. The pyramid also illustrates another idea related to both needs and contributions. Refugees at stage one need more help in services than those who are at stage three, four, and five. Refugees at stages four and five are able to contribute more to American society and require fewer services than those at stages one, two, and three.

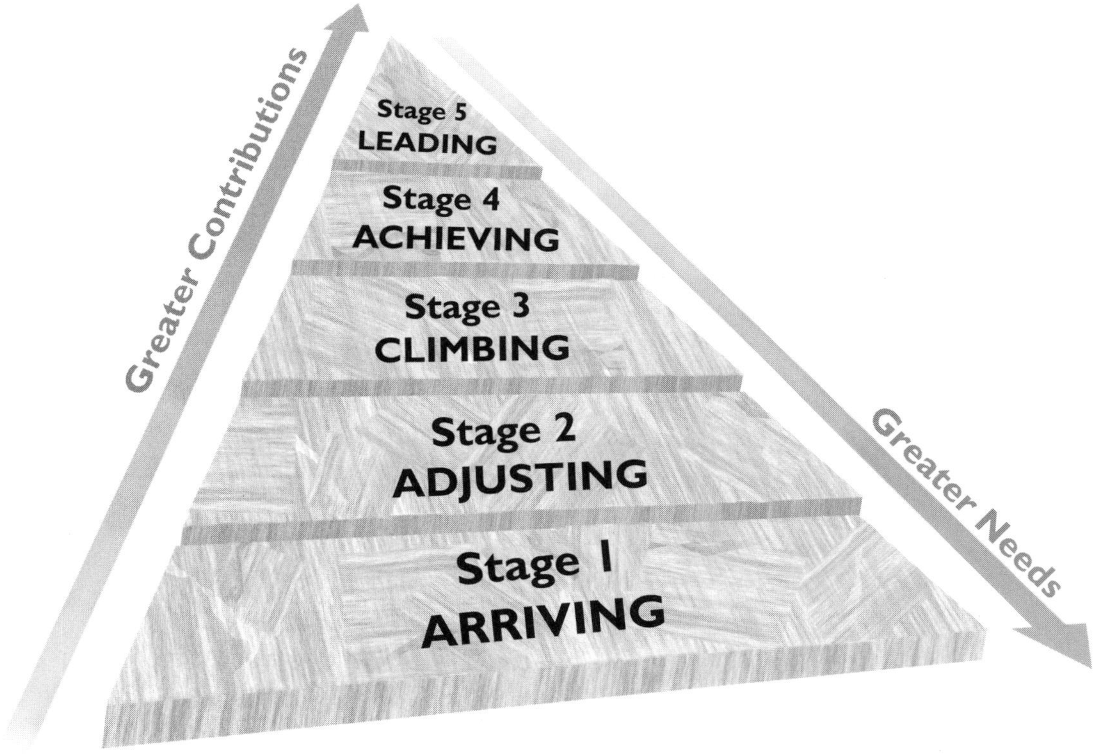

Greater Contributions

Greater Needs

Stage 5
LEADING

Stage 4
ACHIEVING

Stage 3
CLIMBING

Stage 2
ADJUSTING

Stage 1
ARRIVING

Some of my colleagues have noted that there are fewer "mainstream" Americans near the top of the pyramid as well. This is, of course, true—in any community there are usually more followers than leaders. However, I would like you to consider that for many refugees, becoming a leader is an important way to "prove" ourselves in America, and we want to see as many of our family and community members reach this position as possible. For some in the refugee community, this aspiration to lead feels like an important means of proving our capacity to contribute to America—it is not so much a choice as a necessity—while, perhaps because they are born here, it may be that mainstream Americans do not feel this need to "prove" themselves.

A Note on the Development of This Model

I developed this model based on personal experience as a refugee and as a professional working since 1980 with refugees and immigrants in Thailand and America. I have shared these five stages with hundreds of refugees from different parts of the world; most liked the model and felt it would help both refugees in their personal adjustment and development and native-born Americans who work with and help refugee individuals. Many people have encouraged me to share this model with others, especially those who want to improve their services when working with refugees. I hope more and more people use this model as a basic framework when helping refugees and their families.

Some of my immigrant friends with whom I shared these five stages told me that most of the characteristics in stage three, four, and five in this book are similar to immigrants' experiences. You are more than welcome to use them if you think that they are helpful to you and the immigrants you work with.

Five Stages Related to Refugees' Needs and Contributions

As seen in Figure 2, page 35, the five stages of refugee development can be represented as a pyramid. The pyramid reflects both the refugee's reality of upward mobility and the relative numbers of refugees who move into these stages—that is, the higher up the pyramid, the fewer refugees. All refugees arrive at stage one. Many move to stage two. Fewer move to stage three, and so on. For the service provider, this has important implications: a goal is to help move as many refugees as possible to their highest potential. Perhaps as we learn more about how to do this work, the pyramid will not be a pyramid, or will at least show much more room at the top!

The pyramid illustrates another idea related to both needs and contributions—what refugees need at any given point, and what they can contribute. The arrows at the left and right sides of Figure 2 show the relative needs and contributions of refugees.

Refugees at stage one need more help in services than those who are at stage three, four, and five. More services require more money to be spent. Again, look at the contribution side carefully and see that the refugees at stages four and five provide higher contributions to American society and need less help in services than those who are at stages one, two, and three. This reflects their increasing independence and mastery of American culture.

Challenge yourself to find ways to help more refugees move faster to stage three, to become independent more rapidly, and to contribute more to society. The faster we can help refugees become independent after their arrival, the better. Economic realities aside, the feeling of independence and the sense that one is contributing to society are components of good mental health.

Six development patterns

I have noted some typical developmental patterns as refugees adjust to life in the United States. No two refugee individuals' development patterns are alike, but they share many similarities. The shape of these patterns depends on refugee individuals' strengths, capacities, and limitations. (Note that these patterns do not reflect refugees at stage one because every refugee goes through stage one.)

Pattern A—Plateau

Refugee individuals move up to a certain point and stay there for a while, and then they go down to the same place where they started. These refugees stay at the same stage—usually stage two—for the rest of their lives. Refugees who fall in this pattern have very limited capacities, strengths, and resources. This pattern is often seen in the elderly with health problems. Their health problems may prevent them from moving further up the pyramid and may cause them to fall back. Some of these groups of refugees give up their hopes and dreams.

Pattern B—Climb and settle

Refugees who experience Pattern B move up and stay still for a while, then up some more, and then drop back, but not as far back as their starting point. These groups of people often have some English skills or work skills from their previous job. They drop back because they lost their job or experience a family problem such as divorce.

Pattern C—Climb, rest, climb

Pattern C illustrates those refugees who move up and stay still several times. They keep pursuing their dreams even though they face some difficulties in their adjustment and adaptation to the new society.

Pattern D—Spiral up and down and up again

Refugees at Pattern D move up and down, up and down, and then up and down and still up—climbing a little higher with each spiral. Their lives are slightly different from Pattern C. Giving up their dreams is not an option for them. They may struggle with several issues, such as lack of English skills, loss of family members in the new country or in their home countries, or lack of financial support for education or the acquisition of new job skills. Each of these obstacles throws them back a step, yet they keep striving to overcome the new obstacles—hence the up and down movement—but an overall upward direction.

Pattern E—Slow start, fast climb

Pattern E illustrates refugees who start moving up slowly at the beginning and faster after they pass a certain point, such as the development of adequate English skills, the completion of an educational program or securing a job that matches their skills and experiences. Some of these groups of people arrive with some advantages: good education or working experiences with Americans and Westerners in their home countries.

Pattern F—Rapid rise

Pattern F describes only a very few refugees. Typically, these are highly educated people who have lots of experiences and skills. They arrive in the United States with a good understanding of American systems. Most of them received degrees from the United States, went back to their countries, and then returned to America as refugees. Some attended universities taught by American or Western professors abroad. Shortly after their arrival they get their license and move up very fast to a secure, fulfilling job.

Knowing these developmental stages will help those who work with refugees understand both individual refugees and groups of refugees. Of course, some of the developmental stages suggested might not apply to all refugee individuals and groups because not all the refugees have the same life experiences when they come to the United States. Some have experience as farmers and come from underdeveloped areas, and others come from cities and are educated as professors, lawyers, or doctors. Nevertheless, the patterns and stages should give you a general reference as you think about the refugee experience.

The Five Stages of Refugee Development

Let's look at each stage in more depth.

Stage 1: Arriving

Refugees arrive at their final destination, America. Their minds are filled with relief and joy. They celebrate an important achievement in their life—reaching a safer place. They feel that their dream has come true because now their children will have a better life and bright future. At this arrival stage, refugees depend totally on their sponsors, family members, friends, or government benefits. Soon after arrival, however, some refugees begin to miss their homeland and the family members they left behind. Some have a great deal of anxiety due to the many unknowns they face. Others try to forget their former status as government officers, governors, or ministers. At the same time, they face cultural shock because almost everything in America is different from their country or refugee camp. This shock is especially true for the older people, for those who don't speak English, and for those who live far away from their own family or ethnic community.

As the initial celebration and shock wear off, refugees begin to identify and confront the new challenges they face. This is the beginning of stage two.

Stage 2: Adjusting

Refugees confront numerous difficulties in adjusting to a new society. Many have hard times learning a new language, understanding American culture, finding a job, and looking for a home, all while trying to preserve their culture and traditions. These issues compound an existing, difficult issue that has never been eliminated from their mind: the memories of war, persecution, violence, flight, possibly torture, and witnessing killing, or at best experiencing poor health. Some adults take years to learn English and some elderly may only know fifty words of English. Some get lost in the new society because they do not know what to do, and nobody really understands their complex issues or problems. Such issues include day-to-day living, learning new and different lifestyles, changing roles, facing intergenerational conflicts, struggling with barriers to employment, enrolling children in school systems, coping with depression, or experiencing discrimination.

Some refugees are permanently stuck in stage two. For various reasons, they can't find ways to overcome the new challenges—and more new challenges keep piling on. Old challenges they thought they'd mastered recur. It is a difficult stage, yet most refugees manage to master the basic problems of life in the United States and begin to climb the ladder of personal and social success as they define it.

Stage 3: Climbing

This personal growth stage is when individual refugees try to make their futures better. Some get their college degrees. Others upgrade their skills and get better jobs with good pay. A few save money to start small businesses. Elders attend citizenship classes, while children improve their school performance.

This stage is a stimulating time. At this point, refugees have a better understanding of American ways of life, American cultural norms, and American society. At this stage, they see their future more clearly and are basically more comfortable with their surroundings. They have learned how to communicate with others in English. They tend to explore new opportunities by using their strengths and any available resources to achieve their dream goals. However, some lack support and face tremendous barriers. These barriers include lack of language skills, choosing a wrong career path, lack of financial support, stressful family issues, no time and resources, too many things to do at once, or the feeling that they are too old to do new things.

Stage 4: Achieving

Achieving is an exciting stage when refugees start putting their experiences, knowledge, and resources into practice (or business) and start proving that their ways of doing things work. They become successful, stable people because they learn how things work and begin to use their knowledge about American systems. At this stage, some refugees become managers of organizations, companies, or firms. They are directors of nonprofits or they hold key leadership power somewhere. They might have their own businesses and employees. This group of refugees also includes educators and graduates. They are resources to their community. They gain more respect from their own community and begin to gain some from the mainstream community. They become bridges between refugees and American communities.

Of course, the meaning of success—the achievement of dreams—differs from one person to another. For some people, keeping the family together and mutually supportive is the goal. Other goals include the ability to communicate in English, finishing high school, getting a college degree, attaining citizenship, surviving in the new society, supporting children and family, becoming independent of welfare, being self-sufficient, owning a home, seeing their children achieve their dreams, or keeping their culture while adjusting to American life.

Every focus group I conducted for this book agreed that education is key for refugee success—whether the refugee is a young child or a senior. With an education, most refugees experience their own success—big or small—based on their personal dreams and standards. Parents, in particular, want to be sure that their children experience "success." Focus groups also described the successful refugee as a person who was a good role model, could do things by themselves, knew American systems, worked hard, was positive and respected, and helped others.

Stage 5: Leading

Those refugees who enter Stage 5 find that they have become leaders within their refugee communities and often within the mainstream community as well. They are seen as multicultural leaders, able to move between their own culture and mainstream culture and influence all kinds of people. Becoming a multicultural leader is an honor for refugees. This honor does not come easily and only a few people arrive at this stage. They work hard and earn high degrees of respect from the larger community. They are local and national leaders and champions within certain fields where they have worked hard for a very long time. They hold leadership positions in business, government, or nonprofit sectors.

These people become role models in their own communities as well as for the mainstream community. Others recognize them as successful people and can learn a lot from them. Meanwhile, these leaders often feel a need to teach and to help others reach their own goals and leadership potential.

Of course, some refugees think that they are community leaders, but they are not considered leaders by their own cultural community. Other refugee leaders are respected in the mainstream community and disassociate themselves from their own community. These two last groups of leaders are not truly multicultural leaders.

Summary

This chapter briefly described the five stages of refugee development in America and some experiences that refugees have as they move through these stages. Understanding these five stages helps you to plan more effectively and confidently for your future work with refugees. You can use the Five Stages at a Glance (Figure 3) for your quick review and understanding of each stage.

FIGURE 3. FIVE STAGES AT A GLANCE

Stage 1—Arriving	Stage 2—Adjusting
• Refugees arrive at their final destination	• Refugees confront many difficulties as they adjust
• They experience strong feelings of relief and joy	• Language and culture are two major barriers
• The dream of safety comes true	• Refugees may experience difficulty coping with bad memories and loss of family members
• Some refugees feel reborn	
• Refugees celebrate arrival as their highest lifetime achievement	• Problems become more complex and difficult to understand
• Some miss their homeland and family members	• They face countless new and different life experiences
• Some totally depend on others—especially family and sponsors—to help them	• It is difficult to find or keep jobs
• Everything around them seems new and good	• Some refugee children are behind in school
• Refugees learn American norms and learn through observation to avoid mistakes	• Elders may feel lonely and isolated at home
	• Some families cannot find a home to live
• They face immediate needs	• Refugees get frustrated, depressed; some people feel "lost"

Stage 3—Climbing	Stage 4—Achieving	Stage 5—Leading
• Individuals create a personal future plan to build their new lives	• Refugees prove that they can do most things that "mainstream" people can	• Refugees take pride in their successful achievements
• Some upgrade their skills and get better jobs with good pay	• Some become administrators or managers	• They become leaders of both refugee and mainstream communities
• Some get college degrees	• Some become mentors and help others reach their dream goals	• They are "champions" of certain fields—housing, health, etc.
• Refugees improve their understanding of American cultural norms and ways of life	• Some hold leadership positions	• They earn high respect from the larger community
• Refugees are comfortable communicating in English with others	• Some play a bridging role between their own and mainstream communities	• They become role models and mentors for many
• They feel comfortable in their environment	• Some have their own small businesses and hire from within their refugee community	• They are seen as "successful" and others want to learn from them
• Some save money to open small businesses	• They gain more respect from their own and other communities	• They become executives and hire staff beyond their own community
• Children improve their school performance	• Some refugees become resource persons and are active in both communities	• They help others reach leadership positions
• Elderly attend citizenship classes	• They understand American systems better than other refugees	• They understand how systems work for both refugee and mainstream communities
• General understanding of local banking and school systems		
• Some explore possibilities to grow and develop		

Chapter Three

Stage One—Arriving

Imagine yourself in the refugee experience. You have walked hundreds of miles. You have lost friends and family. You have no belongings. You live in constant fear. You have starved. You have suffered illnesses without medication. You have lived underground, out in the rain, at the mercy of thugs. You may have experienced or witnessed violent actions you previously could never have imagined. You have learned you can never go home, and then wait months and years to finally find a new home.

Is it any wonder that most refugees feel a sense of rebirth and relief when they set foot in the United States, or in any country that offers them a new home? For most refugees, this stage is the happiest stage, one that few refugees will forget. After so much misery, these new Americans feel that all the worst is gone and that finally bad things won't be interfering in their lives again. It looks like everything they will have in their future is good for them and their families.

The Refugee at Stage One

There are three overlapping phases in stage one. First is arrival in the new land and the joy that accompanies it. Next is awakening to new opportunities and the strangeness of new surroundings. Finally, refugees experience loss as they recognize how much they left behind.

CHARACTERISTICS OF REFUGEES AT STAGE ONE

- Refugees arrive physically at their final destination
- Their mind is filled with relief and joy
- Their dream of having a safer place to live comes true
- Some feel that they are "reborn"
- They celebrate one of the most important achievements in their lives
- Some miss their homeland and family members
- Some refugees need great amounts of help from others (family, friends, sponsors, community members, resettlement groups)
- Some feel that everything around them is new and good
- They start learning how to behave to avoid mistakes
- They face essential short-term needs and other long-term needs after six months, for both material and emotional support

Like all human emotions, these can happen all at once, in steps, or over and over again. At the end of this chapter you will learn some tips for helping the stage-one refugee live with and move through this stage.

Arrival

While this stage officially starts when refugees and their families arrive at a final destination after a long, exhausting journey, it actually begins earlier. The transition of the refugee into a new life in America begins at the refugee camp, when word finally arrives that the refugee (and perhaps his or her family) can leave. Now the refugee is smiling because he or she has passed a screening process conducted by the Homeland Security Adjudicator and has been accepted to live in a new country (America, for the purposes of this book).

It happens like this: One day the refugee's name appears on a list or is announced by the United Nations staff as a result of their screening process, saying that their sponsor (a family member or voluntary agency) has completed all Homeland Security forms, that they met all its requirements, and now the refugee will be able to leave the camp for his or her sponsoring country at an exact date and time. At this point, many refugees cannot sleep or they collapse in tears because they are very happy about the good news. Others are suddenly sad because they realize some of their friends or family members will stay behind. And even though they passed the test, they are still uncertain about their future until the airplane takes off.

For those lucky refugees who get on the plane, arriving in their new homeland feels like their greatest moment. Some feel it is the safest place in the world. When their sponsors or relatives hold up a sign or call their name, body, mind, and soul are full of happiness, excitement, and enjoyment. At the airport or at their final destination, some refugees do not know their sponsors or how to communicate with them because they don't share a common language. Whatever happens between them and their sponsors, these refugees are still happy because they know they are safer, more secure, and better off physically, mentally, and financially. They are no longer worried about their basic needs—food, shelter, and security—which had been a daily struggle at the refugee camp. It is a time for celebration, and sponsors often host a party for their new arrivals.

At this moment, refugees see everything around them as good. They are positive about their new lives even though they don't know what will happen to them next week or next month. They do not have many belongings with them—each of them holds a small bag—but they are as happy as if they had a million dollars in their pockets. Their smiles reveal hope and confidence.

This "greatest moment" lasts about six months, depending on the individual refugee. For young children, this period stays with them for a very long time and ends after they attend school and face new challenges. For adults, it lasts for a few months, until they face some difficulties in searching out their new lives. For older people, not long after their arrival, they start having a feeling of isolation because they do not even know where to pray or to whom they can talk.

Awakening

After the joy of arrival, the refugee begins to awaken to complex new surroundings. They find that everything around them is different from their homeland—language, behaviors, body language, transportation systems, housing, and appliances. Even simple things are complicated such as when to sleep and when to eat, how to dress for the (usually much colder) weather, or how to get around the neighborhood. Newcomers are confused when interacting with others. They don't know where to find their own traditional foods. They need time and assistance—time to observe and learn about everything around them and someone who can speak their language to show or teach them things they need to know for everyday living. During this time, most refugees learn by observation rather than through instruction.

Let's look at a few of the many adjustments most refugees must make: adjusting to food, to climate, and to time.

Foods

New refugees often cannot find the right ingredients to make the foods they are accustomed to and must adjust to new foods. This was especially true for refugees who arrived twenty years ago, before multiethnic grocery stores became more common. Some people bring their own food to eat because they don't know if they can buy their food here. Of course, these foods last for a short time.

Why is food so important for new refugees? Food can be a major health issue for new arrivals. The human body adapts to food from a particular locale. In this country, many food portions are very large and the diet has a lot of fat, sugar, and salt. The result of an American diet for some refugees is an increase in obesity and related diseases such as diabetes. These diseases were almost unheard of among the same people before they arrived here.

Some refugees, even after many years, say that they never feel full or satisfied after eating American foods. Some refugees won't eat certain American foods because they are prohibited by faiths and traditions. Some, with access to ethnic food sources, have literally never eaten American foods. (My mother is one such example. One of my brothers always jokes at my mom whenever we have a family party that she should try American food because she is an American citizen.)

SIMPLE THINGS ARE NOT SIMPLE

Some refugees do not know how to do what seems like the simplest things. For example, some refugees used firewood to cook in their homeland, and now they must learn how to use an electric or gas stove. Some new refugees are afraid to pick up the telephone because they don't know who might be calling and what language that person will speak. Some have no experience using a phone.

Let me share with you one funny story. In 1996, the wife of one of my friends stayed with us temporarily. She was home by herself while my children were at school and my wife and I were at work. One day, she asked me why I did not pick up my phone when she called me, and I replied that I never heard any phone ringing.

"When did you call me?" I asked.

"Between 10:00 and 11:00 AM today. And I called you five times in the past two days, but you never pick up the phone."

I found this odd, and I couldn't figure out what was wrong with my phone. The conversation happened a few more times during the month, and I began to wonder if she had my work number. Finally, I asked her, "How did you get my work number?"

She replied that I'd given it to her. I didn't recall that, so I asked her what number she was dialing. It was my home number! She had assumed that the same number would reach me at work or at home. It may seem obvious to us that this wouldn't work, but to a person unfamiliar with phone systems, her assumption that a phone number would follow a person from phone to phone is quite sensible.

Climate and time

Coping with a major change in climate is a big adjustment for new refugees at the arrival stage, many of whom come from much warmer places. However, during the first stage, many new refugees do not feel cold because their hearts are warmed! Children, adults, and elders who come to the northern states are excited to see and touch snow for the first time in their lives. The snow helps them enjoy their new life here. When my plane left Thailand in 1993, it was 70 degrees; when I arrived in Minnesota, it was 32 degrees below zero! My family and I did not prepare for this kind of frigid weather because we knew nothing about it. The United Nations provided jackets for us, but even those winter jackets were not meant for subzero temperatures. Climate was the first of many differences we had to adapt to.

After arriving, some new refugees try to adjust their personal sleeping and eating times. Time where they came from might be extremely different from America. For example the daytime here is the nighttime in Asia. This kind of adjustment takes probably three weeks to a month. Also, schedules differ for when eating and sleeping take place. However, refugees have great survival skills. They adjust to the new climate and time rapidly.

Loss

Refugees often feel a sense of loss after arrival. This sense of loss is compounded by social isolation. New refugees face isolation because of language and cultural barriers, lack of transportation, and living far away from their own people. Elderly refugees tend to be the most isolated group because they don't have people to talk to. Some new refugees live in apartments surrounded by people from cultures other than their own. Although it seems they are not physically isolated, they are on a cultural island. Isolation also increases because of the dependence of Americans on the automobile. It's impossible for new refugees to get their driver's licenses within six months or even a year if they do not know English. Without a license, refugees depend totally on their sponsors or family members to take them from one place to another. Some are afraid of using public transportation because they have gotten lost, plus they do not speak English so all verbal directions or written signs are foreign to them.

Success Factors

- Strong support from family, friends, community members, and sponsors
- Receiving basic guidance
- Thinking of America as a permanent home, not a temporary one

Strong support

As mentioned before, some refugees at this stage totally depend on others to help them. They tend to live in areas where their family or friends already live. By living close to their family members and friends, they hope to reduce the barriers of language, culture, transportation, and day-to-day living. New refugees can observe what other refugees do, and their community members can share their experiences as new refugees. New refugees are more comfortable learning from their own people's experiences as they start building their new lives. With all this support and guidance, they feel safer, happier, and more confident in themselves, and these feelings contribute to a positive outlook on their life and future. Emotional support from friends, family, community members, and sponsors plays a very important role in helping a refugee move from stage one to stage two.

Receiving basic guidance

For a refugee, America is a new, different world. America is more advanced technologically than where most refugees come from. To some new refugees—especially those from less technological societies—the new information needed to negotiate American life is vast. To attempt to convey all this information at once is like trying to empty an entire bucket of water into a narrow-necked bottle in one splash. Both the bottle and the pourer will have greater success if the bucket is emptied slowly! So, refugees adjust more successfully when information is taught in simple and step-by-step instructions, followed by simple examples to make sure that they really understand. Of course, some refugees arrive from countries with similar levels of technology or have prior experience in Western methods and culture. For these, the transition is closer at hand.

Thinking of America as a permanent home

New refugees will have greater success if they can concentrate all of their efforts on rebuilding their future in America from the very beginning. Focusing on the past can destroy their ability to move forward. Refugees must move forward even though it is hard for them. Therefore, refugees should think of America as their permanent home, not their host country. Dreams of near-term returns home, while normal, can distract them from the task at hand—building a life in America. It is impossible for them to go back to their homeland at this time and only a small number of refugees go back to live in their homeland after they become U.S. citizens.

Remember, most refugees arrive with their body first and adjust their mind later. Those who would help refugees adjust successfully can do so by providing appropriate ways—culturally and spiritually—to help them detach their mind from their home country so it joins their body here, now, in America. Refugees that connect with their own ethnic community, join cultural activities, and learn new things will have more success easing their mind into their new home.

Challenges

At stage one, most refugees face the same types of challenges regardless of their country of origin. Communication is difficult, and adults, in particular, may take more time to learn or improve English skills. Transportation is very troubling; some lack driving skills suitable for the United States. Refugees at this stage need full support from many sources because they are new to America's environment, culture, and systems.

Challenges include

- Difficulty in communicating and interacting with others
- Finding basic necessities such as food, clothing, and shelter
- Lack of transportation or fear of traveling alone
- Trouble adapting to the new environment and culture
- Dealing with overwhelming issues

Communication

As mentioned, many new refugees do not speak or understand English well. Those who do not know English may be afraid to talk to others, meet others, pick up a phone, or leave their home because they are unable to communicate or interact with others. Even those who know some English may not understand American conversational English, which is very fast and clipped.

Finding basic necessities

Finding food, shelter, and other basic needs is hard and is a big job for some refugee families. Finding available and affordable housing is also a big challenge for new refugees, especially those who have many members in their family. A few new refugees become homeless again just months after their arrival because they can't find affordable housing. Larger families face challenges finding room for the entire family, and some wind up with two parents and several teens living in a one-room apartment. This challenge becomes more severe for those who have no family members or friends to help out.

Transportation difficulties

Lack of transportation is a major barrier for many new refugees. They do not have a car. They do not understand public transportation systems. They don't speak English. They do not know directions to their destination or cannot read directions in English. They fear getting lost.

Adapting to a new world

Imagine that you are coming from a remote countryside in Africa, Central America, Asia, or Eastern Europe, and now you land in a big city in America surrounded by new people, a new culture, a new language, new markets, new school systems, new ways of living, and so on. What do you see for yourself? Many new refugees face just this experience. This adaptation is a major challenge for most refugees. However, refugees know how to survive in extreme situations. They can quickly adjust to the new environment, especially if they are young.

Dealing with overwhelming Issues

Dealing with overwhelming issues in their new life is one of the major challenges faced by new refugees. Some lack appropriate coping skills or have difficulty developing them. Those who become overwhelmed may give up their hopes and dreams. They may stop working to achieve the things they planned to do for themselves and their families. Some do not know which issue they should take care of first, second, and so on. Those who have success with this challenge tend to tackle things little by little, taking time to process so they don't feel overwhelmed.

What Refugees Need at Stage One

At this stage, refugees depend totally on family members, sponsors, friends, community members, social service providers, government agencies, and others to help them survive. They have nothing, so they need everything from everybody.

Obviously, refugees are concerned for their futures and the following questions are raised by most new refugees: Where can I find a job? What should I do for my career? Where is the closest ESL (English as a second language) class? Where can I find cultural activities for my parents or my children? Some new refugees need information regarding welfare benefits or locating people who can help them with translation or filling out forms. Some new refugees want to find housing and they do not know how to do that. Even if they have a big family here, the family cannot support the new refugees indefinitely.

There are two kinds of assistance needs for the new arrivals and their family: 1) immediate needs for today, this week, and this month, and 2) longer-term needs. Immediate needs include advice about what kinds of foods they should or should not eat; appropriate clothing; and how to use the bathroom, kitchen appliances, telephone, television, and so forth. The most critical need is applying for public assistance. Longer-term help is needed for tough challenges such as looking for jobs, finding schools for their children, attending English classes, finding housing, or learning who to call for help. If their own family sponsors them,

Title VI of the Civil Rights Act of 1964

"No person in the United States shall, on ground of race, color, or national origin, be excluded from participation in, be denied the benefits of, or be subjected to discrimination under any program or activity receiving federal assistance."

Refugees should be informed that they have the right to ask for an interpreter if they need one. Both federal and state laws recognize the rights of limited English speakers, but these rights too often are overlooked.

that's a great benefit because they speak the same language, and more importantly, they can depend on them for a time. If not, adjustment is more difficult, particularly with culture and language differences. For example, when refugees start talking about finding a job or finding (or resuming) a career, they get depressed because their English language skills are not as good as they believed them to be back in their homeland.

Dealing with poor health, new environments, culture and language barriers, everyday problems, or social isolation may lead to depression. And later on, depression may lead to a major mental health issue for some refugees, which you will learn about in detail in the next chapter.

Immediate needs

- Educate refugees about day-to-day activities and skills
- Explain appropriate and inappropriate behaviors
- Explain United States currency and how to properly spend money
- Provide furniture, appliances, and other basic shelter needs
- Explain how to use the telephone and utilities such as electricity and gas

- Take refugees to grocery stores, especially to seek out their traditional foods
- Help them apply for welfare benefits
- Show them how to use public transportation
- Provide translation and interpretation assistance
- Provide clothes suitable for the climate (especially winter)
- Help children get physical check-ups and immunization shots before they go to school
- Help children enroll in school and help them with the English language and homework
- Provide translation and interpretation at hospitals if necessary

Needs after six months

- Help parents with their children's school conferences
- Help adults find English as a second language (ESL) classes
- Help adults get their driver's licenses
- Help adults find jobs
- Take the elderly to meet their own people or to places where they can practice their religious beliefs
- Provide families with resources when they ask for assistance

Keep in mind that some new refugees arrive with their families and others are individuals—including children who arrive without a parent. Single women often arrive with large numbers of children. The needs of each refugee differ widely, as do the needs of each group of refugees.

Summary

After a long journey—from escaping wars and persecutions to living in the refugee camps—refugees finally reach a place of comparative safety. They start their new life with few resources and little knowledge of America. Most refugees cannot communicate in English and do not know where to begin once here. People who want to help refugees should help them address both immediate needs and needs they have after the first six months.

Tips for Stage One

For New Arrivals	For Those Who Help New Arrivals
• Celebrate and enjoy a great achievement in your life	• Allow new arrivals to celebrate and enjoy their new lives
• Be open to learning new things by observing and listening to others	• Provide new arrivals with simple instructions and show them basic life skills such as using a stove and electricity
• Be positive about your new life and feel comfortable about new things around you	• Do not bombard new arrivals with too much information at once
• Ask questions first before doing things you don't know, such as how to use a stove or electricity	• Be supportive by providing translation or transportation
• Ask your sponsors or family where you can get help when needed	• Take them to meet other community members and friends
• Learn the value of a dollar, how to use currency, and how to go shopping	• Bring new arrivals to the welfare office and help them apply for public assistance
• Learning English is your first priority and will help you look for a job to support your family	• Bring them to have a physical check-up at a public health department or a hospital
• Apply for public assistance	• Bring their kids to have immunization shots before starting school
• Look for an affordable home	• Help parents enroll their children in school
• Have someone teach you how to use public transportation	• Help them find affordable housing
• Ask your sponsors or family members how to enroll your children in schools	• Take them with you when shopping or going to the grocery store

Chapter Four

Stage Two—Adjusting

NOT LONG AFTER THEIR ARRIVAL, refugees and their families start searching for ways to rebuild their lives. They face new challenges every step of the way. During the adjusting stage, refugees realize that they have more problems and difficulties than they first thought—from finding jobs, learning a new culture, and understanding American systems. These challenges and difficulties go beyond language and cultural barriers, and their complexity often makes it difficult for others to understand or empathize. Most refugees turn the challenges and difficulties they face into new opportunities and creatively build their new lives. (Note that not all refugees face all the challenges mentioned in this chapter; as with the rest of the book, these are general observations.)

The Refugee at Stage Two

Stage two begins when the "honeymoon period" of arrival ends and refugees try to find their own new path. At this stage, new arrivals start feeling exhausted, depressed, frustrated, hopeless, and lost.

Due to multiple stressors, the adjusting stage is a challenging stage. Some refugees take years to move from this stage to the next one. They confront all kinds of difficulties adjusting to a new society while searching for answers for their new lives here in America. Refugees must learn a new language, understand American culture, fit into a

Characteristics of Refugees at Stage Two

- Refugees confront numerous difficulties in their adjustment phase
- Refugees face many barriers, including language and culture
- Refugees have a hard time eliminating their old, painful memories and grieve over the loss of or separation from family members
- Adjustment problems become more complex and more difficult for outsiders to understand
- Refugees face countless new life experiences
- Some children are behind in school due to language barriers and lack previous formal education
- Elders are isolated and lonely at home, and some have poor health
- Some families cannot find housing
- Refugees are frustrated and depressed; some lose their sense of self, their self-esteem, sense of competence, and so forth

new society, find a job, and look for a home—all while preserving their own culture and traditions. These new issues often exacerbate old ones, which may have never been eliminated from their minds. They are still coping with countless memories experienced in the past such as escaping wars, persecution, and violence; witnessing killing; or suffering poor health. Not surprisingly, depression can be an outcome of these multiple stressors.

Younger refugees usually can adapt rapidly to American society—and children adapt most rapidly. They learn English in a short period of time—months to a year. In contrast, adults take years or decades to learn English and fully understand American cultural norms. In some cases, older adults speak only their traditional language while their grandchildren speak English. This makes communication between generations difficult. Young refugees often become alienated from their traditional culture. This causes elders, who often hold on to the culture of their homeland, to feel isolated from others, including their own children. A few believe that their children do not take care of them well. Elderly refugees are essentially exhausted from dealing with a new diet, isolation, and a new culture.

Some refugees get "lost" in the new society because they do not know what to do, and nobody really understands their problems. These people need extra help from their family members, sponsors, friends, and community organizations. They must share their problems with others and seek help in restoring their sense of dignity and confidence. The risk of getting "lost" increases when refugees do not get help. Most of these "lost" individuals have come from an underdeveloped country or they are uneducated. In general, prior education is a major factor leading to success in America.

Success Factors

- Strong support from community organizations
- Learning English
- Maintaining forward movement
- Persistence
- Keeping goals simple and achievable
- Willingness to seek professional help
- Focusing on building the future; not thinking too much about the past

Strong support from community organizations

At this stage, refugees will do better if they get support and assistance from their own community groups or ethnic organizations. Usually, such community organizations provide culturally and linguistically appropriate services for new refugees. These services help new refugees learn how to obtain the social, health, financial, and other assistance they need. Such services can help them find success dealing with complicated issues such as youth and gang violence, children and education, intergenerational conflicts, authority, immigration issues, child protection, and so on. Refugee-led organizations play a significant role in making connections between their own people and mainstream organizations and, thus, are thus a significant contributor to the success of new refugees.

Learning English

Every refugee must have English skills, and this must be their first priority. The ability to speak English is a primary success factor in the United States. Learning English requires time, patience, and commitment. Refugees who do not start to develop this skill early will have to deal with the problem every day. For every refugee, English is a key for many doors—from going to school and earning a degree, to getting a better paying job, from communicating with their own children and others without fear, to making their life better and brighter. New refugees should know or be informed that English must be their first priority.

Maintaining forward movement

Moving refugees forward quickly from stage two to stage three is one of the factors that will make refugees more successful in their life. Pushing refugees to pass stage two requires lots of energy and resources at the beginning. However, if these refugees stay at stage two, society will later spend even more resources. Stage two is a big and deep hole where refugees can easily get stuck. Pushing and pushing the refugees ahead is an appropriate way of moving them toward self-sufficiency and independence from government assistance. If they remain in stage two long, they may never move to self-sufficiency or independence. It is important to make sure that refugees are moving past stage two.

Persistence

Moving through stage two is a hard and difficult job for every refugee, but they will be better if they do adjust and move on. Persistence pays off. Most refugees in established refugee communities have already been through this, so the new refugees can learn from their predecessors' experiences.

Keeping goals simple and achievable

Setting simple and achievable goals is one of the success factors for refugees. Refugees have to develop one or more goals in order to move to the next stage faster. Any goals that they set must be simple to implement, and each goal must be achievable within a specific time frame. This enables refugees to build a track record of success and a sense of personal competence in the new environment.

Willingness to seek professional help

Seeking professional assistance at an early stage, before challenges feel insurmountable, is one of the success factors that refugees should keep in mind. Refugees should not try to handle everything by themselves. There are many people who want to help, but the refugee must be willing to talk about his or her issues, concerns, or problems. In some cultures, people are not comfortable sharing their personal or family problems with people outside their own family. Keeping things within the family has many merits, but it may also inhibit people from seeking help.

Focusing on building a better future

Success is aided when refugees and their families have a vision of a better life. Of course, their lives are safer now as compared to life in refugee camps or in their own county, but safety alone is not a vision. It helps to have a mental map of the future and the roads they will travel to reach that future.

Challenges

I have heard hundreds of stories about experiences that refugees have gone through after their resettlement in America. Children, adults, and elderly refugees who came from different parts of the world share these stories. In fact, at stage two refugees are facing tremendous challenges no matter where they come from. Some of their stories are more painful to listen to than others. They always talk about their language and cultural barriers, difficulty in finding housing, getting off of welfare, feeling isolated, having no time for themselves, keeping their family together, feeling mistreated by others, their lack of confidence, and so on.

Yet all is not bad. Refugees also share that they enjoy their opportunity, freedom, and safety—things they have here which they either lost or never had in their homeland.

The typical challenges refugees face include

- Language and cultural barriers
- Culture shock
- Lack of transportation
- Stark geographic change
- Change in traditional roles
- Intergenerational conflicts
- Barriers to employment
- Concerns about the future of new generations
- Racism and discrimination
- Health problems

Language and cultural barriers

Language and cultural barriers often prevent refugees from doing everyday things. Knowing the English language and cultural norms can help refugees communicate with others, find a job, travel from one place to another, get a driver's licenses, attend school, help their children with homework, fill out important forms, get promoted, and upgrade their skills. Refugees can become frustrated and depressed because these two major barriers limit their capacity to do things they want to do and things that they know they could do if the barriers were not present. Many times they feel powerless. Every refugee needs these language and cultural skills to succeed in America.

Understanding the English language and American culture helps new arrivals adjust to everyday activities—from interacting with others to behaving "properly" in their workplaces. One poignant example has to

MISINTERPRETATION

Here's one example of an activity that is easily misinterpreted by a health care worker. A Vietnamese common remedy for an illness involves rubbing the location of the illness (chest, back, forehead, neck, stomach) with a spoon or a coin and some type of warming oil until bruising results. This kind of cure is said to work by ridding the child of the "wind" that has caused the illness—a cold, sore throat, stomach pain, backache, headache, or flu. Bruising is an effect of this and can be mistaken for child abuse.*

* From http://www.health.qld.gov.au/multicultural/cultdiv/vietnamese.asp.

do with child rearing. Some refugee parents have problems with the authorities because they don't know American cultural norms about spanking children as a form of discipline. In some situations, this action can be considered child abuse here but is the norm in the refugee's homeland. Some parents feel bad because they simply want to help their children behave in ways that are consistent with their cultural norms and heritage, but in some cases certain cultural practices result in intervention by child protection agencies or authorities. This happens because refugee parents do not understand the child protection system here and because the child protection system does not understand the cultures of the refugees it is serving. In some cases, parents wind up abdicating their parental authority out of fear of losing their children.

Cultural differences are confusing, of course, and in some cases the language differences alone are enough to cause confusion. For refugees, learning English is the key to many doors. A good command of English helps refugees receive and provide job instruction, go to college, sell products, communicate effectively with others, and see their future more clearly. English skills help them solve many problems as well as eliminate most communication barriers. Some refugees share that in American, a person who doesn't know English feels both blind and deaf. So, they need to have good English skills to succeed both personally and professionally. Therefore, refugees must make learning

English their top priority because English is a means to achieving personal, social, and financial goals. For some adults, improving English fluency is a lifelong task. Others describe that they are able to increase their English speaking skills within five years of their arrival. Remember that younger refugees learn English a lot faster than the older ones. Children and young adults learn English in months to a year while older adults take years and decades to gain this fluency.

Culture shock

Immediate culture shock is a common problem that every new refugee faces. There are few refugees who realize the extent of this kind of problem. Most newcomers do not anticipate the shock or understand that it comes from many different factors—discomfort with things around them, noticing how people behave differently from them, the unpredictability of their lives, lack of English language skills, and cultural barriers. Sometimes culture shock causes depression, and depression adds to the feeling of being lost in the new society. Eventually understanding language and culture helps refugees eliminate some of the cultural shock.

LOST IN TRANSIT

I have heard many stories about refugees getting lost on public transportation for hours. Sareth, a refugee from Cambodia, can now joke about her initial experiences using public transportation from home to school and back during her first three months in the United States. She got lost for two to five hours regularly in the first month when she used public transportation. She could not communicate with bus drivers or people who traveled with her. She could not read signs, plus she did not know where the bus was headed. What she remembered were bus numbers and stations, but sometimes she picked a wrong bus. On the bus, she always worried about getting lost. If she did not see her stations or destination, she would just sit there until the bus driver stopped and finally asked her to get off. For months she carried that awful feeling of being lost.

Lack of transportation

In their home countries, some refugees traveled by foot from one village to another. While others lived in large cities, refugees still can have problems negotiating a new transportation system. Language and communication barriers also limit their ability to get a driver's license, read signs, or communicate with others.

Having one's own transportation or knowing how to use public transportation are bridges to help refugees succeed. Riding a bus is easy for people here but not for the new refugee who speaks no English. Most elderly refugees neither drive nor have a spouse who drives. They have to depend on their children whenever they want to go to somewhere. What happens if their children work two or three jobs and have no time for them? In the winter or in bad weather, they have no choice but to stay home surrounded by four walls, which leads to boredom and isolation—one of the causes of depression among the refugee elderly population.

Stark geographic change

Some refugees hail from very small villages where their families had farmed for generations. Farming was their career or work. But farming in America requires different skills. The large-scale farms in America are completely different from the subsistence farms in the homeland. Plus, most refugees initially choose to live in cities where they are close to public transportation routes, social service providers, jobs, and affordable housing. These factors force them to change from farm to factory, from small village to big city, from a simple life to a complex one. They once lived with their own small group of people, and now they are mixed with many people, stacked one on another in a big apartment complex. One friend—who lives in an apartment building about half occupied by Serbian immigrants and refugees—plants a garden on a lot near the complex. She relates a time when a new neighbor woman, who spoke only Czech, came over with some excitement and could name all the vegetables growing in that garden in her own language. The green growing things were universal, and the broccoli looked like a lost friend to her. She was trying to get used to a service-related job when her real expertise was soils and gardening.

Change in traditional roles

A gender role reversal might be the last thing that refugees think they'll have to deal with in a new country. In some cultures, "good" husbands work outside the home to support their families while wives stay home to take care of their families or do housework. Back in the home country of these individuals, women have little decision-making power because of their cultural practices or social norms.

This tradition is hard to maintain once in America. Often, both husband and wife must work outside the home to survive or to make their lives better. Women's roles and power are changed when they go to work to support their families as men do. Men and women have equal roles, responsibility, and power. In some cases, men cannot find a job and they end up staying home while women work. At this point, their roles are completely reversed and women have more decision-making power than men. Conflict often occurs when men want to keep their power or they do not want to give more power to women. Both sides get frustrated and they start fighting to control each other. In the worst case, if their problem cannot be resolved, they add divorce to everything else they have to adjust to in American life.

Intergenerational conflicts

Intergenerational conflict also comes into play in refugee families. In America, refugee parents often lose control because their children quickly learn English and can talk to people their parents can't. Some children use their language power to manipulate their parents' behavior. As mentioned in the section on language and cultural barriers, American laws and norms regarding spanking and similar behaviors can have bad consequences. A child may intentionally or unintentionally alert authorities about a parent's traditional disciplinary action without a real understanding of the consequences to the parent, the family, or the child himself or herself. The children's greater language facility only heightens the power differences and intergenerational conflict.

The situation is complicated. In some cases real abuse (by any culture's standards) may exist. In others, the Americanized children simply don't want to do what their parents tell them to do and act out. For example, some cultures do not allow girls to go out with boys because it is taboo, but the Americanized children want to date in ways that violate their cultural community's values and norms. In other cases the children are right; some parents are too strict in their old traditions and don't learn new parenting skills that fit their children's Americanized culture. The upshot is intergenerational conflict where none had existed, and months and years of difficult adjustment for parents and children.

Also, in many refugee homelands, elders are revered. Elderly refugees often feel that they have lost social and economic status in America. They feel powerless because they depend on their children and grandchildren for physical, social, and financial support. Some refugees do not want their parents to stay with them; instead they put their parents in nursing homes or in public housing. Some elders worry most about dying outside the home and away from their families.

In time, there is an increasing level of conflict between parents and their children due to growing cultural differences. The elderly stick with their old traditions and culture, while their children and grandchildren are increasingly "Americanized." Parents expect their children to maintain their culture and traditions, while children value more elements of mainstream American culture. Most adults and elderly refugees have high expectations of respect from their children and grandchildren, but some children do not do what their parents want them to do; instead they threaten or abuse their parents if their parents discipline them for their bad behaviors.

Barriers to employment

Finding a job is critical for every refugee, educated or uneducated, professional or unprofessional. Some refugees arrive with job skills and training, but some refugees have limited skills, limited English, little cultural training, or little money when they come to this country. The language barrier is a common problem faced by refugees, as mentioned in the discussion of language and cultural norms. English language proficiency helps refugees upgrade their skills, expand their opportunities, and find jobs. The common barriers are:

- Poor English skills or lack of appropriate English skills
- Past experiences that simply do not relate to the new society
- Little or no education
- Lack of opportunity for training or advancement

Sometimes those who do not have high levels of education or who have fewer job skills find a job faster than highly educated refugees because there is less competition in the area of low-paying jobs and foreign academic degrees are not recognized in the United States. Refugees who were professors, doctors, lawyers, or government officials in their home country are unable to find a job at the level that they're used to because professional jobs here require certificates from American universities or institutions. A very small number of refugees who were once doctors or lawyers in their country of origin become doctors or lawyers again in this society. They are now older and funding education to upgrade their skills, knowledge, and licensure is hard. Tragically, their skills can't be used or are under-used, so they end up working as assembly-line workers, janitors, or taxi drivers. These people are immediate assets to American society, yet the system prevents them from adding their professional skills to their new country.

Discrimination and racism are also employment barriers for refugees. Some employers do not want to hire refugees. These employers may have had bad experiences in the past, negative perceptions of a group's work ethic, or do not know certain refugees' culture well.

Concerns about the future of new generation

Refugee parents worry most about the future of their children. Two areas top the list of concerns: educating their children and helping their children avoid gangs and gang violence.

Children's education

Refugee parents hope their children will obtain a high level of education because they understand that the future is limited for those who drop out of high school and have no college degree. By dropping out of school, children not only upset their parents, but they also have to work hard to survive when they become adults. Children often lack financial support because most refugee parents arrive with empty hands. They also lack guidance because their parents are unfamiliar with education systems in the United States.

For example, in some refugee homelands, refugee parents were accustomed to the school making decisions about their children's education. But in America, parents are expected to take the lead in making choices for their children. So, schools in America become frustrated with refugee parents, who, from the school's perspective, aren't taking control of their child's education. Further, parents who do not speak English may never attend school conferences, since they can't understand the conference. These choices can mistakenly be interpreted by the school as lack of concern.

Some children were born in and grew up in refugee camps. These children arrive in America as teenagers with no English language training and no formal education. The school system here puts children into classes based on their ages, not their knowledge or prior education. Put

CHILDREN'S EDUCATIONAL BARRIERS

Most refugee children are smart, and they do great at school even though their English is not as good as other students. But some do not do well because of several factors:

- Lack of English proficiency due to their age or years in school

- Limited or no educational experience in their homeland due to civil war or life in a refugee camp

- No motivation, guidance, or support from parents because their parents do not have time, do not know the school system well, have come from a country where the school system bears this responsibility, or they, themselves, have no education

- Schools lack the knowledge, skills, time, or funding to help refugee children with their needs

yourself in this child's place: you spend five hours a day in a classroom with twenty-five other kids, most of whom were born in America. You know only a few words in English and have had no formal education because you were born in a refugee camp. When you get home from school, no one in your family can help you solve the social or educational problems you face at school. Even if the child has had some education and some English training, the American education system is difficult to negotiate. In some countries, children are placed in grades based on their knowledge, not age. Even when a refugee-camp child has had some schooling, the training level of a fifteen-year-old refugee is not the same as a fifteen-year-old American who has had continuous schooling since the age of four.

The roles of refugee-run organizations become increasingly important to help both parents and children in such cases. Through the assistance of these organizations, refugee parents understand school systems better and increase their participation at schools, and children improve their school performance as well.

Youth violence and crime

Some refugee parents are worried about the danger of gang violence, drugs, and crime. They also worry about their inability to influence their children's choices and actions. These criminal issues will quickly lead to imprisonment and deportation if the children are not U.S. citizens. Refugee youth who are not naturalized citizens are at risk of being deported back to their home country if they commit just a minor crime. Hundreds of refugee kids are in federal prisons waiting to be deported back to their parent country. For example, there are hundreds of Cambodian youth in prison who now face deportation to Cambodia, a country that they have never known because most of these youth were born in refugee camps in Thailand.

Refugee parents express concerns that their children have too much freedom compared to the past and they do not want to listen to their parents anymore. Other parents share that they do not have good relationships with their children because their children do not listen to them and they have no right to discipline them. Some youth abuse their parents.

Racism and discrimination

Some refugees report that mainstream Americans discriminate against them because they do not speak English well, because they are different, or because they are refugees. Other refugees feel that they are judged as ignorant people. Refugees who experience discrimination share that they feel shocked, depressed, afraid, and unsafe. They find it hard to eliminate the experience from their heart. Whenever a new incidence of discrimination happens to them, they have a flashback to what happened to them in the past.

Racism and discrimination issues create a no-trust wall between refugees and non-refugees. Most refugees fear authorities, mistrust their government, and do not understand American justice systems. Educating refugees at an early stage about their rights and introducing them to how the American justice system works might help them in the long run.

A poem written in 1991 by Rafael Amor of Zaire sums up the refugee discrimination experience:

Do Not Call Me Stranger [14]

DO NOT CALL ME "STRANGER" because in a mother's love we all receive the same light; in their songs, their kisses, close to their breast, they all dream about us being equal.

DO NOT CALL ME "STRANGER" Do not think of where I came from. Better to think of our common destiny and to look at where time is leading us.

DO NOT CALL ME "STRANGER" because your bread and your fire assuage my hunger and my cold, and because your roof shelters me.

DO NOT CALL ME "STRANGER"! Your wheat is like mine and your hand like my own! And hunger, never overcome, wanders about everywhere constantly changing its victims.

And you call me "stranger" because your way drew me and because I was born in another country; because I have known other seas and

---

[14] From "What Lies Ahead: Listening to Refugees." Leicester, England: Christians Aware, 1992. Poem written by Rafael Amor. See http://www.christiansaware.co.uk.

have sailed from other ports. And for all that, the handkerchiefs that wave to tell us goodbye are all the same, and the same also the retinas moistened by the tears of those we leave behind. The same are the prayers and the love of those who dream of our return.

DO NOT CALL ME "STRANGER"! We all cry with the same voice and share the same fatigue which we carry about since the beginning of time when frontiers had not been invented, well before the arrival of those who divide and kill, of those who sell our dreams and would, one day, invent the word "stranger."

DO NOT CALL ME "STRANGER"! It is a sad word, a cold world, evocative of exile. Do not call me "stranger"! Watch your son run with mine, hand in hand, until the end of the road.

DO NOT CALL ME "STRANGER" because they understand nothing about language, about frontiers, about flags. See them go up to the heavens: a single dove carries them united in a single flight.

DO NOT CALL ME "STRANGER"! Look at me straight in the eye, beyond hatred, egotism and fear and you will see…I cannot be a stranger.

—Rafael Amor, Zaire

Health problems

As noted earlier, lack of food, medicine, and water, and experiences with torture, sickness, and depression from a long stay in refugee camps are common among refugees. These factors lead to physical and mental health problems among refugees, especially the elderly. In addition, some health problems are new developments in the new homeland; for example, more Somali elders have diabetes due to the inability to digest refined sugars and other foods and the lack of exercise and social activities.

Some refugees do not want to share their health problems with people other than their family members, including doctors. Others have never visited doctors or have had no physical check-up for years. Others don't believe in Western medicine or standard American medical practices and have their own systems of medicine. Sometimes the health care system does not provide them with accessible services, either linguistically or culturally. Some diseases did not exist in the refugees' homeland. For some cases, the refugees' culture might have had a different explanation for the illness, and this can lead to increased misunderstanding about health problems when refugees and American health care providers try to communicate.

What Refugees Need at Stage Two

Many refugee community leaders and members report that refugees often turn to each other first before seeking help from outsiders and mainstream institutions. Others share that they help each other by providing emotional help; sometimes financial support; help with daily needs such as translation, transportation, or organizing a social event; and sharing time and possessions. Most refugee societies are collective groups, so if one person fails the other members in the group will try to help them get back on their feet again. This is one of the reasons why refugees prefer to live close to their cultural communities.

Typically, refugees go to a family member and then to a community leader, clan leader, or elder for help with any sort of problem. After exhausting the above sources, they seek assistance from people known to them in their social network. Finally, they seek institutional support from public and private sources.

The following are common needs of refugees and their families at stage two. Note that some of these overlap with needs in stage one.

- Health education and health prevention programs
- Transportation
- Translation
- Mental health education
- Stress release programs for the elderly
- Finding adult classes in English as a second language

- After-school tutoring programs for youth
- Help with understanding mainstream culture and cultural norms
- Help with immigration application or paperwork
- Assistance in looking for jobs
- Help with purchasing a home

Summary

Stage two is a critical point for the refugee's experience in America. If refugees can meet multiple challenges and find solutions as they adjust to a new culture, they can advance personally and professionally. Challenges are diverse and subtle and depend on the age, educational background, services received, family support, and home culture of the refugee. For this reason, no single set of guidelines applies to their experiences or the kinds of help they need. It is important to listen to and understand the individual stories, backgrounds, cultures, and needs of refugees at this stage. The community that receives the refugees—and especially those individuals and organizations that help the refugees in stage two—must learn about this stage, assist and aid where possible, and come to understand the new neighbors or community members as the potential assets they are.

Tips for Stage Two

For refugees	For those who help refugees
• Think positively about your new life here	• Try to understand refugees' problems through their story telling and nonverbal behaviors
• The new challenges you face are only temporary, and you are not alone when you face them. Support each other as much as possible	• Provide refugees with advice, support, and assistance in dealing with everyday life and American ways of life
• Have physical checkups regularly and follow the doctor's recommendations	• Help refugees better understand and trust the banking system—to use the banks rather than hiding money
• Talk to sponsors, family members, and friends about your problems	• Remind refugees to take care of themselves—going to see doctors, allowing time for exercise, and eating the right foods
• Seek professional help if you think that your feelings (your emotional state) are not normal or you feel depressed	• Help the elderly deal with social isolation and depression
• Get a driver's license as soon as possible and save money to buy a car	• Refer refugees to available resources for themselves and their family members
• Attend English as a second language (ESL) classes to improve your communication and English skills	• Provide transportation assistance or help getting their driver's licenses
• Look for a job. Consider that public assistance is temporary, and you must become self-sufficient as soon as possible	• Help them to enroll in English as a second language (ESL) classes
• Focus on school because education is key to your future success and for your children's success	• Help refugees with their resume, understanding the interview process, or applying for their first job
• If you are a parent, learn new parenting skills to help children deal with two different cultures	• Volunteer to help children improve their school performance through tutoring or after school programs
• Comply with all immigration laws and requirements	• Help parents with translation at school conferences
• Make contact with others to explore your future opportunities	• Teach refugees about American culture or how to interact with Americans
• Make friends with Americans and learn more from them about how they interact with others or about their culture	

Chapter Five

Stage Three—Climbing

DURING THE CLIMBING STAGE, refugees look for possibilities, opportunities, and potential that can help them grow, climb higher, or otherwise make their lives better. Some do better than others based on their strengths, capacities, skills, and resources. Refugees use all the resources they have to accomplish their dreams and goals—to build better lives. Ideally, if they pass this third stage, their lives or the lives of their family members will become a lot better and easier than they were at stage two.

The climbing stage demonstrates both an opportunity and a challenge faced by refugees. This stage is different from stage two, where refugees had to deal with many challenges, yet had few opportunities. During stage three, refugees experience about half challenge and half opportunity. Most refugees are actually dealing with two stages at once—stages two and three. They grow while they continue to adjust and adapt. Refugees now become more Americanized as they adapt to American culture, norms, and lifestyles. They play active roles in helping their immediate community. Most importantly, they begin making contributions back to their new society. This is one clear distinction from stage two: stage three refugees are no longer dependent on their host families and sponsors.

CHARACTERISTICS OF REFUGEES AT STAGE THREE

- Refugees create their own personal, future plan based on their hopes and dreams
- Refugees upgrade job skills
- Some get better jobs with good benefits
- Some earn college and technical degrees
- Refugees understand American cultural norms better
- They know and adapt to American ways of life
- Refugees can communicate in English with others more comfortably
- They show comfort with surrounding environments
- Some refugees save money to buy a new home or open a small business
- Children improve school performance and completion rates
- Some refugees attend citizenship classes
- Refugees understand local banking and school systems better

As they grow, refugees start thinking about developing their own plans for the future. They assess their language ability and other strengths—physical, mental, and financial—to find out what they can or cannot do. After putting their future plans in their heads, they share them with family members, close friends, or sponsors. Finally, they begin implementing these plans by starting with a single step based on their internal strengths and capacity. Refugees' individual plans, of course, differ from one to another and depend on their family values and specific hopes and dreams.

As refugees start seeing their future more clearly in their imaginations, they also realize that they have the capacity to do something for themselves, their families, and even for their community. They are positive about their new lives, and they know more about ways and resources to help fulfill their hopes and dreams. Some find themselves doing the same things differently, while others learn from entirely new experiences.

The Refugee at Stage Three

The primary feature of a refugee at stage three is hard work to accomplish many things at once. At this stage, refugees start to integrate into their new society and become productive citizens. They go back to school to upgrade their skills or to earn college degrees. Others move to new jobs with better benefits. Some learn American systems and become leaders within their own community. A few start their own small businesses. Elders attend citizenship classes to prepare themselves to be American citizens, while youth improve their academic performance.

As noted earlier, most refugee parents focus their goals, hopes, and dreams on their children. Parents provide their children with emotional, moral, and financial support and they make sure that their children have higher educations. Most refugee parents believe that a higher education will help their children to have better futures. Some parents work two or three jobs to support their children's education.

When dealing with difficulties, some refugees see their new situations as similar to their worst experiences—the extreme life or death situations that they went through in the past. Others are positive about their lives in the new land and culture. Refugees often consider that their new plans are their new life journeys, and that they must implement them slowly, carefully, and patiently. Refugees know that this new journey may be long and difficult to achieve. Also, they must learn how to balance their own personal life, work, family, and the level of involvement with their immediate cultural community. Besides their personal motivation, commitment, and family support, refugees at stage three get outside support from different groups of people—sponsors, friends, community members, and institutions.

Refugees use their internal strengths such as dreams, self-motivation, commitment, and desires as well as outside support to reach their goals. It is still hard for individual refugees to do many things by themselves even though they are strong or know how to move from one stage to another. There are few refugees who are able to move to stage three while they are at stage one and stage two. Those who can move most quickly are educated, have good language skills, or have previously worked with Americans or Westerners in the past.

By stage three, many refugees are

- Making more money by working more than one job (especially true for those who do not arrive with good education or job skills)
- Improving their communication skills
- Getting a higher education with hopes that their future will become better
- Sending their children to colleges to fulfill their dreams
- Upgrading their job skills in order to make their job easier and to be more effective
- Moving to better-paying jobs after learning more skills
- Becoming leaders in their ethnic community and bridging two cultures and communities
- Utilizing their newly developed skills to help other community members
- Opening small businesses (if they were able to save some money at stage two)
- Buying their dream homes
- Becoming United States citizens

Success Factors

Many factors help refugees find success as they climb into American society. Several stand out:

- A positive outlook
- Self-discipline and commitment
- Good health and resources
- Hopes and dreams for their children

Positive outlook

Refugees in stage three still face numerous barriers even as they begin to experience some very great successes. Refugees who succeed find that keeping a positive outlook when facing obstacles keeps forward

MY OWN STORY

Some of my refugee friends said that I was lucky when I was selected to join with eleven Southeast Asian refugee leaders in the Bicultural Training Partnership (BTP) program in 1993. I participated in this BTP project less than six months after my arrival in the United States. I was new in the country and knew nothing about how this program would help me, but one of my brothers, who worked with a refugee-run organization, encouraged me to be part of the program. After a detailed explanation by my brother, I decided to apply for the program. In my imagination, even before I joined the program, I saw this BTP program opening a door for me to grow. So, I dropped my classes at a technical college and accepted the BTP offer.

I made the right decision. BTP opened the door for me to get my post-secondary education. At the same time, I gained management consultant, leadership, and cross-cultural communication skills. BTP paid for all of my undergraduate program tuition, plus it provided me with a part-time job. Thanks to those who designed this special program to help newcomers like myself, BTP was one of the avenues that helped me grow, showed me how to climb higher, and, more importantly, assisted me to go beyond my personal stage three in a short period of time. As I look back, I can see that I went through stage one, two, and three at the same time, and, in part, this was possible due to the Bicultural Training Partnership.

I hope to see more programs like this one. BTP was a special project of the Saint Paul Foundation, with the Amherst H. Wilder Foundation and Metropolitan State University as collaborative partners. The program began on January 1, 1993, and ended in 1996. BTP had two main goals: to strengthen Southeast Asian organizations and communities and to begin to define a functional blend of Asian and Western ways of conducting business and serving community needs.

momentum going. Refugees themselves should see their new life as a positive one and their new world as an opportunity for them. They also should celebrate their small successes when those successes come.

Self-discipline and commitment

Self-discipline and strong commitment are two fundamental factors that help prevent refugees from giving up their goals, hopes, and dreams while they face critical challenges and barriers. Self-discipline helps refugees to stay focused and follow through with their plans. Commitment helps refugees to keep doing what they are doing even though some interruptions occur. These two factors mentally remind refugees to work harder and have more patience in order to make their hopes and dreams become reality. Working in the daytime and going to school at night is normal for refugees. Those who lack self-discipline and commitment will easily give up their future goals due to the many challenges, barriers, and unexpected problems that happen to them or their family members. Self-discipline and commitment have to come from refugees themselves.

Good health and resources

At this climbing stage, refugees need not only to have high self-discipline and commitment but also need lots of time, good health, and resources such as financial aid or loans; health care; housing; employment information; immigration legal assistance; and social services for elders, youth, and families. The more resources available for them, the faster they can move to the next stage. Without these, refugees might fail along the way. Refugees have to understand that if they want to grow, they must climb up because if they don't climb up they won't be able to have better lives. Knowing about and being able to access resources is a real power for refugee success.

Hopes and dreams for their children

Some refugee parents may never move beyond stage three, but they help their children to do better and grow or they push their children to climb higher. For these parents, an important aspect of stage three is pushing their children forward to accomplish things they recognize they may not be able to accomplish themselves. Refugee parents often motivate their children to take advantage of the opportunities they have in America, which were unavailable in refugee camps or in their own countries. Some motivate their children to excel by pointing out their own weaknesses such as limited capacity to grow or a bad working environment. Others set higher standards or expectations for their children when children begin to develop their own future goals.

We have seen that some families in refugee communities have neither high school diplomas nor college degrees, but their children have higher educations or become successful due, in part, to their parents' hard work.

Challenges

A mountain climber needs strength, skills, an understanding of the geographic area, and good weather. Like mountain climbers, refugees face a lot of challenges in this climbing stage. They may not have enough strength, resources, or know-how, or they may not have anybody to guide them. Sometimes all these deficits are combined. Some refugees have tried hard to climb to the top but they have never made it. Others climb halfway and fall down back to stage two. Not everybody who wants to pass this stage succeeds.

Obstacles in stage three include:

- Continued language barriers
- Lack of a clear career plan
- Lack of life balance
- Lack of a support system
- Lack of financial and academic support
- Family troubles in the homeland

Continued language barriers

At stage three, lack of English language proficiency limits refugee advancement when pursuing a higher education or doing other things they want to do. The language barrier is very much like a chronic disease that refugees have to deal with every day and everywhere they go, especially when they must communicate with others in writing. Language barriers often put refugees in disadvantaged situations.

Some adult refugees at this stage know how to speak English well, but they still lack written communication skills. In order to be an effective supervisor or to attend college, refugees must have both oral and written communication skills.

Lack of a clear career plan

One of the greatest frustrations facing refugees in stage three is when they put their time, energy, and resources into the wrong career plan. Some refugees can't find jobs after finishing their degrees. Others never use the degrees that they have earned to perform their job functions. Some careers can't be found in the areas where they live or some can't find jobs they really enjoy. For example, a refugee from Sierra Leone, Africa, said that he could not find a job that fit the degree that he pursued for years, so he had to go back to school to start his career plan over.

Some refugees do not plan for their future or a career. They think that their current jobs are permanent. Sometimes it is easy to find a job after their arrival because of the high demand for labor and a good economy. Refugees may not consider the consequences if they are laid off fifteen years later. No job is secure today, so refugees, like all Americans, have to think and plan for a changing career that fits the future job market. This is hard for any person—and much harder when one does not fully understand the culture.

Some refugee youth do not know what to do after finishing high school because they do not have somebody in their family to guide them. They may go to college and take classes and then change their major one or two years later because they find out that the classes they took do not help them reach their career goals. So, they must start their classes over. By the time they finish college, they end up with more debt than their friends plus they waste their time, energy, and resources.

Lack of life balance

In order for refugees to overcome the many challenges and barriers they face, they have to do many things at once. Often the hard work of building a new life in a new country leaves little time for themselves or their families. Personal success does not always guarantee family success. Lack of life balance can lead to divorce, accidents, or poor health. These things turn refugees' lives upside down and interfere with their goals.

Let me share with you a story of a refugee who had worked very hard for fifteen years after arriving in America—twelve to fourteen hours a day, six days a week. He believed that working hard was the only way that he could catch up with friends, especially those who had a higher education or their own business. Over time he accumulated a lot of money, a big house, and an expensive car—but he had no life.

It is good for refugees to try doing things they want to do, but they must make sure that they have time to relax and be with their family. If they don't, they might be considered careless family members; their spouse or children might not be happy with them because they are not with their family when they need them. Sometimes, they forget about taking care of their own health. So, all refugees need to learn how to balance the demands of self, work, family, and school—and this is especially critical at stage three.

Lack of a support system

At their workplaces, refugees need different kinds of support from different people: their employers, supervisors, coworkers, and even administrative systems. In most cases, refugees are stuck with their low-paying positions because they do not have support systems that provide opportunities to grow or to get promoted. Often, refugees are hired as frontline staff to work directly with their own refugee community members. Only a few refugees are hired to fill upper-level management jobs.

In stage three, refugees need refugee-serving organizations to provide both technical and moral support for refugee employees. Refugees need help understanding American work ethic, policies and procedures, appropriate behavior, expectations of being good employees, and other American cultural norms. They need to be shown ways to improve themselves or available resources to help them grow. The primary support systems most refugees need are from their own cultural groups.

Lack of financial and academic support

Lack of financial and academic support prevents refugees and their children from moving up. Higher education expands their ability to grow. If they lack both supports—financial and academic—they will not have opportunity to move up. Children whose parents are struggling in stage two sometimes cannot pursue their higher education because their parents need them to work in order to support their family.

Receiving bad academic advice is also a common experience shared by refugees. A refugee from Chad, Africa, told me that he spent five years to finish a degree that he already had from his homeland. He found out later that he could have attended only some classes and completed his American degree in two years.

Fear of using the financial aid loan system also is a barrier for refugees. Many refugees have successfully finished their higher education because they were not afraid to take student loans. These loans and financial supports, in combination with making education a priority, help from their teachers and academic advisors, and good advice from community leaders and mainstream advisers, can help refugees overcome educational barriers.

Some younger refugees have too much fun and forget their future. They see only today but not tomorrow. For example, they love their car but not school. A successful factor for youth and children is education; from some refugee parents' perspectives, no education means no future.

Family troubles in the homeland

One frequent barrier that prevents or slows refugees from moving from one stage to another, especially from stage three to stage four, is when the situation worsens for family members back in their home country. Remember that most refugees have two homes: one is America and another is still their country of origin. Bad situations in the country of origin always affect a refugee's ability to grow in America.

Individuals with two countries frequently share their resources and feelings with their families who were left in the homeland. Their minds are

REFUGEES TALK ABOUT EDUCATION

NOU VANG, a Hmong woman and refugee from Laos, came to America at the age of six. She explained how and why she went on to earn a master's degree: "Financial aid definitely made it possible for me to achieve my family's dream of me going to college. We were poor and wouldn't have otherwise been able to afford tuition. I also had great teachers who consistently recognized and affirmed my own potential and cheered me on. I wasn't even thinking about graduate school when I finished my bachelor's degree, but my advisor strongly encouraged me to apply and reminded me that I had something to contribute to the world."

BORIS (he did not want his last name used) came to America as a refugee at the age of 56.

In Russia he had been a chemical engineer and owned a locomotive company. He believes in education (and loves it) and attended classes at Portland Community College in Oregon. He said he wanted to learn as much as he could about everything to help him better understand American ways of life. Boris used what he learned at school to help his refugee community members, his family, and especially elderly friends.

DR. TUYEN NGUYEN, a refugee from Vietnam, writes: "Work part time, study full time. Don't be afraid to get a loan for your education. Hang on to your dream. Reading is key to success. Invest in your education and future."

with their families because their families there do not have safe places to live, lack financial resources to support themselves, or have no way to survive without the refugee's incoming financial support. Almost every refugee family here sends money to support family members in their home country. Since this support is a matter of life-or-death for their families, refugees send much of their income home rather than spending it on their own personal or professional development.

When the situation back home gets worse, refugees split not only their financial resources into two parts, but their minds and hearts as well. When this happens, their ability to grow is affected because they can't fully concentrate on implementing their desired plans. Often their climb in stage three goes slower or takes longer than they planned.

Some refugees completely give up their dreams after bad situations happen to their families in the homeland. Others stop for a while and then restart. They may do this several times until they successfully meet their goals, and then they can move to stage four.

What happens to those who completely give up their dreams? They may go back to stage two and stay there for the rest of their lives, and their lives will never become better. In some cases, this consequence impacts their children's lives, too, because their children do not have role models to help guide them. For children, if there is nobody in their family who paves the way for them, some end up the same as their parents—never passing stage two.

HOPES AND DREAMS AT STAGE THREE

After talking to hundreds of refugees through focus groups and interviews, the following are common hopes and dreams of refugees at stage three:

- Family members stay together
- Ability to communicate with others in spoken and written English
- Earning college degrees
- Passing citizenship
- Surviving in the new society
- Supporting children and family
- Helping children to get a higher education
- Having a stable job and good pay
- Independence from welfare assistance
- Standing on their own two feet
- Having their own transportation
- Having their own house
- A better or easier life

What Refugees Need at Stage Three

Each individual and group of refugees has different needs. Women are struggling with defining their new roles in the new society. Children are confused about their identity, their parents' expectations, and their own goals. Elders may feel hopeless about their lives and future. Some needs persist from stage two, plus:

- Youth need all kinds of encouragement, academic help, and financial aid to achieve their academic goals

- Youth need guidance in developing their future educational goals

- All ages need motivation

- Adults who wish to open small businesses need help developing their business plans

- The elderly need transportation to and from hospitals and translation services when there

- Families need help with immigration matters and paperwork to sponsor their family members

- Individuals need help to improve their speaking and writing skills

- Individuals need better understanding about American systems and how to access resources

- Individuals need support from different groups of people in order to achieve their future goals and to move beyond stage three

Summary

Refugees who have made it to stage three have already come through the pain of the escape, the camp, and the cultural shock of a new country. They have learned untold ways to adapt and somehow still desire a higher level of success. This stage is where that higher level of success can happen given the right luck, good health, and an adequate system of social support. This chapter has enumerated universal pressures or barriers at this time—elements to the refugee story that might help anyone understand this stage better. Refugees in stage three must overcome barriers such as a lack of support, a lack of life balance, lack of clear planning, and troubles with their families in their country of ori-gin. For those who would help refugees adjust and thrive in America, understanding stage three is key, and through this understanding refu-gees' life journeys may be made easier.

TIPS FOR STAGE THREE

For refugees	For those who help refugees
• Take care of yourself and make sure that you stay healthy	• Remind refugees to take care of themselves or to slow down if you see that they need to relax
• Learn to balance needs of self, family, and work	• Try to understand refugees' strengths and assets when you help them
• Develop educational goals—get your higher education and look for scholarship opportunities	• Provide refugees with clear guidance and options in developing their new career plans
• Upgrade your skills—job skills, communication skills, and social skills	• Help them improve their communication skills, especially written and oral language skills
• Look for new jobs that support your future goals	
• Get out of public assistance and stand on your own two feet	• Provide refugees with information so they are able to access different resources
• Plan your lifelong journey and implement your plan with patience and care	• Support refugees when they are new to their job or when they are stuck in low-paying work
• Use all your strengths, assets, and support systems to achieve your goals	• Refer refugees to the right people with the right skills when they need help
• Do not let bad situations back in your homeland drag you down, ruin your future, or make you feel hopeless	• Educate refugees about American systems and appropriate ways of doing business in the United States
• Get your citizenship, if time permits	• Help them get their citizenship
• Get involved with your refugee community and learn more from others	• Provide them with resources so they can get licensure and certificates faster
• Provide moral support to other refugees and let them support you too	

Chapter Six

Stage Four—Achieving

STAGE FOUR, ACHIEVING, is an inspiring stage where refugees (who, at this point, sometimes prefer to be called New Americans) start putting their experiences, knowledge, and resources together into practice. At this stage, New Americans are competent in their work and in fulfilling their job functions. They feel that they are successful personally and professionally, financially and academically, culturally and socially. They are knowledgeable about American systems—education, government, business, or nonprofit. They know where to get resources to help their own ethnic community as well as other refugee communities, and they have become mentors and leaders for their own people.

During this stage, some refugees or New Americans might become managers of organizations, agencies, or companies. Some have their own growing businesses and employ their own people. New Americans gain more respect from their own community, from other refugee communities, and from the mainstream community. They become bridges between refugee communities and mainstream American communities.

The Refugee at Stage Four: New American

At stage four, refugees improve their cross-cultural communication, supervision, management, and leadership skills. They are comfortable with American systems. New Americans provide evidence that they

Characteristics of Refugees at Stage Four

Refugees or New Americans have the ability and know-how to do the same things that native-born Americans can do

- Some become mentors and help their own refugee people reach their dream goals
- Some become administrators or managers in nonprofit, government, and private business
- Some hold leadership or mid-management positions
- Some play bridging roles between their own refugee and mainstream communities
- Some have their own small businesses and hire their own people to work for them
- Some gain more respect from their own and other refugee communities
- Some are active in building refugee communities
- Some become resource people for their own community or organization
- Most understand American systems

are successful, stable, and secure people financially, economically, and professionally. This group of people no longer consider themselves to be refugees because most of them have become U.S. citizens. Some are active in the American political process or become advocates for refugees. They don't see themselves as much different from other mainstream people in terms of skills and expertise. They are knowledgeable about how to work with both refugees and non-refugees. Some become managers or administrators in mainstream organizations, companies, or agencies. Some hold leadership positions, such as key managers or executive directors, in their community-run organizations.

How does this stage differ from stage three? At stage three, refugees try to build their personal skills, knowledge, and expertise in order to make a living more easily. At stage four, New Americans prove to themselves that they can do things that most native-born people do, plus they start helping their own refugee friends reach their dream goals. One main difference, then, is this element of reaching beyond self to others, reaching out with newfound skills to help their community.

Individual refugees have different concepts or marks of success. Some want to make more money because they believe that money can buy possessions—they want a big house, nice cars, or expensive jewelry. Some want honor, name recognition, and fame. Some want control, which they find as managers, directors, or business owners. Some want to obtain more knowledge so they select higher degrees of education as their mark of success. Therefore, money, possessions, prestige, control, and knowledge are each milestones of success for different individuals.

At stage four, New Americans have a lot to offer both refugees and mainstream culture. They have many good stories to tell us, especially about how they reached this point from empty hands when they arrived.

Successful New Americans seem to share certain attitudes. They view each day as a fresh beginning in their lives. They do things they deeply believe in. They keep their minds open to what they believe. They see their work primarily as service to others, not as a means to their personal benefit. They develop their willpower based on their inner beliefs. They set themselves increasingly difficult goals, and then persevere until each of them has been achieved.

> From the refugees' perspective, a successful person is a person who is able to attain both individual success and success for his or her family. This means that individual success is just not enough; refugees feel a responsibility to help their family too.

At stage four, a successful person is the one who is recognized by his or her own community as a real asset. This person is well known and respected by his or her own community. Other people in the community want to be like him or her. He or she always helps people achieve their future goals by providing resources and being a role model, mentor, or manager, or by owning a business and employing his or her own people.

From the refugees' perspective, a successful person is a person who is able to attain both individual success and success for his or her family. This means that individual success is just not enough; refugees feel a responsibility to help their family too. Within some groups of refugees, the successful person also has to sacrifice their time, energy, and resources to help their entire refugee community.

Success Factors

Many factors and strategies help New Americans move out of stage three to a point where they feel at home with mainstream culture and are able reach out and help others effectively—to be part of stage four. In some cases—such as training prior to arrival in America or length of stay in America—the factor is one over which the New American has little influence. In others—such as developing a strong support system or consciously learning to live in two cultures—the New American exercises much more control. These factors and strategies include

- Length of stay in America
- Maintaining a positive attitude
- Building a strong support network
- Developing effective communication skills
- Transferring knowledge and skills
- Becoming self-reliant
- Learning to live in two cultures
- Walking the extra mile
- Recharging energy
- Learning to lead

Length of stay in America

Most New Americans have spent at least fifteen to twenty years in America before reaching stage four. This time frame varies from individual to individual. Many New Americans spend decades working hard pursuing their dreams of becoming successful people in American society. Some families of refugees take more than one generation to reach stage four. Grandparents may stop at stage three but they support their children or grandchildren to go to stage four and beyond. Problems with English fluency, education, and training may hold one generation back but be overcome by the next.

Related to length of stay, the age at which a refugee enters the United States influences development. As noted earlier, the younger a refugee comes to America, the faster they adjust to the new society and are able to move through the stages of development. The concept of "learning curve" could be substituted for length of stay. Younger refugees learn and adapt more rapidly—they have a shorter learning curve because they enter at an age when they would normally have also been "learning the ropes" of their own homeland's culture, so such learning is natural. Older refugees take more time to learn the same material and begin achieving success because they've already passed the time in life at which one normally learns about cultural norms. Some refugees reach stage four in a shorter period of time after their arrivals. This group of refugees usually has more of the success factors mentioned above. For example, recent refugees from Kosovo grew up in cities, received Western-style degrees, and have found it easier to adapt to American life.

JOBS HELD BY IMMIGRANTS, BY LENGTH OF TIME IN UNITED STATES*

Position	Median Years in U.S.
Management, administrative	20.5
Precision trades (electrician, mechanic, baker)	13
Professional (teacher, engineer, nurse, doctor)	11
Clerical (bookkeeper, bank teller, office support)	11
Driver, machine operator, assembly work, labor	9
Technician (lab worker, company programmer)	8
Service (maintenance, cook, nursing aide)	8
Sales (includes cashiers and store proprietors)	7

* Paul Mattessich, "Speaking for Themselves: A Survey of Hispanic, Hmong, Russian, and Somali Immigrants in Minneapolis-Saint Paul" (Saint Paul, MN: Wilder Research Center, November 2000), 12.

Holding a positive attitude

A positive attitude helps New Americans stay motivated when they feel down. It is one of their survival skills, and it helps them achieve their goals. The necessity of a positive attitude is always on the mind of New Americans, and it reminds them that they have to feel good about their new lives here even while they have to deal with the realities of life, with difficulties, or with things beyond their control. A refugees's attitude can also be influenced by the actions or support of the people surrounding them, such as parents, relatives, friends, or sponsors. Through a positive mind-set, New Americans see their lives clearer and brighter even while facing numerous challenges.

Building a strong support network

As stated in stage three, getting support from family members, friends, sponsors, community members, social service providers, government agencies, and others is very important for the success of New Americans. Strong support is just as critical in helping New Americans reach stage four. The earlier they receive this support, the swifter their progress. This support can be emotional, technical, financial, and political, based on what the individual needs. In stage four, New Americans need more political and emotional support from their own refugee community leaders and mainstream community leaders.

Building networks and connecting with other community leaders is one of the supporting strategies among New Americans. They become stronger through their networking. New Americans increase their skills through sharing information, knowledge, resources, and business practices. Networking, relationship building, and connecting with others—both other refugees and native-born Americans—help New Americans become successful.

Developing effective communication skills

Communication skills include conversing, writing, and making presentations. Like most managers, executive directors, or key leaders, New Americans need strong communication skills in order to interact effectively with their communities and in their workplaces. Remember that one of the barriers preventing New Americans from succeeding with their future goals is a language barrier. At this stage, refugees do not usually have difficulty speaking English, but they face communication barriers due to their communication styles and approaches. That is, even though the New American may speak English well, he or she may not really understand the nuances of communication. These style differences can be pronounced and have an impact on how well a New American can communicate with mainstream leaders. (You will learn more about these differences in Chapter 8.)

Some older New Americans communicate well with their own refugee community members but not with mainstream people due to their native accent. In contrast, many younger refugees are fluent in English but not in their own language. This becomes a real challenge that mainstream employers have to sort out when selecting new employees.

Most New Americans have developed strong cross-cultural communication skills—a real benefit for their employers. They are competent in these skills due to their own experiences living in two cultures at once. To succeed, they have identified and bridged gaps that otherwise would cause misunderstanding between two cultures when working together. This cross-cultural communication skill is a real plus for the New American and for his or her workplace colleagues.

Transferring knowledge and skills

Many refugees arrive in America with well-developed, transferable knowledge and skills—bankers, doctors, lawyers, professors, government officers, and engineers. Such skills enable the refugee to move faster from one stage to another because these skills are needed in American society.

Some New Americans arrive with high degrees of education from their own or other countries (including America). In cases where the degree is not from an American institution or from an institution recognized in America, New Americans usually have to upgrade their skills and knowledge before the degree will be recognized here. When the degrees or certifications are not recognized, some former educators and professionals cannot use their skills and expertise. They end up underemployed. But even though their skills and knowledge can't be transferred, this group usually adapts faster than those people who arrive without some higher education, certification, or profession.

Becoming self-reliant

As New Americans become more self-reliant, their motivation is reinforced. Even in adversity, such as job loss, most New Americans never give up their hopes of regaining self-reliance. Some learn from their previous mistakes and correct them. Some believe in working hard. Some learn something new to improve themselves by attending classes, reading books, or volunteering in community activities.

These people have clear goals for their future and know where they come from and where they are going. They get jobs as soon as possible to support themselves and their family. They work full time and go to school part time or go to school full time and work part time. Above all, they create positive attitudes toward their self-reliance and never allow

LEARNING TO LEAD IN A NEW LAND

Afeworki Ghiorghis is a former supreme court judge from Eritrea. He left his country ten years ago when the war between Eritrea and Ethiopia started. Now he is a U.S. citizen living in the United States. He has eight children—three live in the United States and five live in Eritrea. All of his children are adults. Afeworki left behind everything he had. He has hoped that the border conflict between Eritrea and Ethiopia would be resolved and that together the two countries would live in peace as good neighbors. He sometimes dreams of going back to his country.

In the United States, Afeworki has volunteered to help his Eritrean community as well as other refugee communities by using his legal and judicial experience. More importantly, he has helped his community build unity. Afeworki shares his thoughts and plans for the future of his country; his Eritrean slogan, "One People, One Heart"; his Eritrean history, culture, and tradition; and his hope for his own community here in the United States. He wants his community members to love and help each other, to unite as one community, to promote women's roles, and to help their homeland of Eritrea.

negativity to drag them down. From New Americans' perspectives, developing confidence in one's self is a necessary step in developing self-reliance. They established clear goals when they arrived, and as each goal is achieved, they reinforce their belief in their capacity.

Learning to live in two cultures

Living in two cultures is not simple; it requires a high level of under-standing of both one's own culture and the mainstream culture. New Americans are proud of living in two cultures. They take advantage of their cultural strengths and blend them with the new culture when creating their new path. Being able to keep both cultures is one of their measures of success.

At stage four, New Americans are very comfortable with mainstream cultural norms and systems. They have also become experts in specific fields and in working with their own cultural community and other refugee communities. They have high competence in communicating and working with diverse groups of people, and they use their cross-cultural working experiences and intercultural skills appropriately. Some are fluent in both languages—their own language and English.

The elder generation of refugees in all communities is happy to see their children keep both cultures and languages. However, some young professionals give up their culture and traditions and focus their career development solely on mainstream culture. Some parents share that they feel they have made a mistake by not finding ways to help their children keep more of their cultural values and identity.

Walking the extra mile

Most New Americans have to walk the extra mile in order to catch up with the rest of the society. This attitude of walking the extra mile is accepted as a moral standard by many New Americans, especially those who are at stage four. They work longer hours. They do more than their assigned jobs. They mentor others and help build their refugee community. They are actively involved in the American political process. Some spend time educating non-refugees about their community and culture.

They are community leaders. Some become board members of mainstream organizations as representatives of the refugee community.

Why do they do all this? Most New Americans or new community leaders are afraid of failure. They have two different jobs with two different bosses: a formal "job" with someone who signs their paychecks and an informal "job" as a representative of and to their own refugee community. Playing this bridging role requires more time, energy, and work. Some feel that they have an obligation to help build their own community after work or on weekends.

Recharging energy

New Americans can run out of physical, emotional, mental, and spiritual energy as they work to keep up their commitments. Yet they need energy to keep moving or pursuing their dream goals. Think of this energy as the "battery" that fuels the New American. Because the New American faces multiple, complicated challenges, the battery drains quickly. If New Americans do not have enough of energy they will burn out quickly. New Americans ought to commit themselves to take care of their body, emotions, intellect, and spirit. Relaxation techniques, proper diet, exercise, and good family support all help recharge energy. Whatever they choose to do, New Americans are going to succeed at a better rate if they combine work and outward success with some kind of process of recharging their batteries.

Learning to lead

As New Americans become leaders in their cultural communities, they help other refugee friends achieve their personal goals and help build the whole refugee community. In order to do all of this effectively, New Americans need to spend time, energy, and personal resources to develop or improve their skills as effective mentors and leaders. They need to learn such skills as leadership development, community organizing, collaboration, advocacy, and using American political processes to influence their community.

But for some New Americans in stage four, becoming an effective leader in the cultural community is not enough. New Americans who have learned to live in two cultures can also learn about mainstream leadership styles from native-born Americans and then blend the two styles, approaches, and practices when creating a personal leadership style. In some cities, programs have been set up specifically to help with this process. For example, in Saint Paul, Minnesota, three programs—Bicultural Training Partnership (BTP), Southeast Asian Leadership Program (SEALP), and New-American Collaborative (NAC)——were established to help refugee community leaders increase their leadership capacity to work effectively with their own people, mainstream people, and American systems. Most of the participants of these programs were key managers and executive directors from nonprofits and a few were from government agencies and corporations. These three programs not only helped New American leaders to increase their leadership skills and competence, but also motivated them to actively participate in civic engagement and in systems change.

There are three significant roles that New American leaders can play as leaders:

- They can empower others to take more active roles in building their refugee community by providing technical assistance or mentoring activities.

- They can help others gain more knowledge and skills through community building workshops or training.

- They can bring in resources—information, expertise, and money—from outside to help their own refugee community.

Challenges

Challenges always remain with refugee community members and leaders at every stage of development. At stage four, New Americans face several challenges. These challenges are difficulties in applying knowledge and skills, balancing personal and family success, high expectations from their own refugee community, and wrestling over power.

Difficulties in applying knowledge and skills

New Americans often face difficulties when applying their unique bicultural knowledge and skills to working with their own refugee community or to working with native-born Americans. Sometimes, their refugee community does not accept the New American's ideas. Other times, the mainstream community does not appreciate the New American's dual roles and special insights. However, New Americans have an opportunity to play a bridging role and eliminate some misunderstanding. The New American can apply bicultural skills to help both communities increase their mutual understanding and acceptance of each other's values.

Here is a typical barrier: Sometimes the New American's community chooses to stick to its traditional ways of working, refusing to learn new things or refusing to change practices. This becomes a major challenge faced by New Americans, now leaders, who try to use their mainstream skills to help their own people for the best interest of their community. As a result, some New Americans say that they find it easier to work with native-born Americans or the younger generation of refugees versus the older generation. Some executive directors of refugee-run organizations report this experience. They have gained a lot of knowledge about nonprofits from mainstream organizations, but they have difficulties in working with their refugee board of directors. Some of their board members just do not want to learn new things that can be applied in American society, or they retain traditional ways and never want to change.

Resistance also exists in mainstream organizations. Particularly in non-profit workplaces, but also in corporate settings, mainstream employers say, "We love different perspectives." This phrase sounds beautiful, but it is only meaningful when people have motivation to accept new ways of working or when they really want to learn from refugee perspectives and experiences. What happens if they are just saying they love different perspectives but really do not want them? The New American shares his or her perspectives and ideas, only to find that the mainstream ignores, rejects, or even penalizes them for sharing exactly what the employer requested! The mixed messages that New Americans experience can be disheartening.

In theory, the New American's ability to apply the skills they have learned from mainstream leaders to help their own refugee community sounds very good. Likewise, the New American's capacity to apply what he or she has learned when working with refugees to the needs of mainstream organizations is a wonderful idea, too—in theory. Knowledge and skills should move across cultural divides, and most people think this idea makes a lot of sense. But the reality is that the New American is going to have a difficult time applying his or her bicultural insights in both the refugee community and mainstream community. Nevertheless, it can be done successfully!

Balancing personal and family success

As with stage three, the pressure of balancing personal life, career aspirations, and family needs continues, and worsens because in stage four, the New American is serving his or her own refugee community and being a bridge to the mainstream community. As a result, some new Americans are very successful in their personal or professional lives but not in their family lives, while others are not so successful in making money but are able to spend more time with their family. The pressures to earn money are severe, though, and many family stressors result: children drop out of school, spouses ask for divorce, and the family becomes unsettled. Thus, the family risks that became noticeable during the climbing stage can become worse during the achieving stage.

High expectations from the refugee community

The refugee community has high expectations from its leaders. In each refugee community there are just a small number of leaders who are at stage four. These leaders have to decide how involved they would like to be in their refugee or cultural community. There are hundreds of events and invitations each year—funerals, weddings, cultural events, fundraisers, serving as panelists, and being advocates.

A refugee community needs leaders and leaders need community support. This reciprocal relationship is always in the mind of New Americans. However, the leaders have to ask themselves a critical question of how much time, energy, and resources they can invest in their community and how they can respond to high expectations of their community. Good leaders always step in when their community needs their political, moral, financial, and technical support.

Wrestling over power

Power struggles among community leaders is a common issue in refugee communities. Sharing power does not happen easily when community leaders do not want to work together because of clan or tribal systems, regionalism, gender, resistance of others, lack of leadership skills, and so on.

Conflicts or frictions can occur when different groups (or the leaders of those groups) do not agree with each other's ideology and agendas. Conflicts also occur due to the backgrounds of various types of leaders in each refugee community.

A typical power struggle occurs between younger generation leaders and older generation leaders. On its face, such a power struggle can appear to be simply young versus old: the older generation of leaders wants to keep their power as long as they can, while the younger generation of leaders wants to earn more respect and be recognized by the older leaders. But the reality is more complex than that. Older leaders often think that younger leaders are not yet mature and too Americanized, while the younger leaders believe that the older generation is too inflexible and traditional to be effective leaders.

Regardless of the source of the power struggle, it looks bad for a community if fighting for power continues unabated and unfazed by outside intervention. In more successful leadership settings, good leaders put the needs of their community ahead of their own personal power. Leaders work together for the best interest of their own communities. The older leaders nurture the younger ones so that by the time they retire, the younger leaders are ready to lead. Each group of leaders needs the other and to respect and recognize each other for their contributions to their community. This is the ideal that leaders in stage four need to strive for.

What New Americans Need at Stage Four

It is common for mainstream society to expect a New American to reach a high level of development and then to reduce the support given to them. Lack of support from America's larger institutions in assisting New Americans to become successful before, during, and after stage four is a common issue. Glass ceilings are real barriers for New Americans and always prevent them from growing. So, New Americans need a lot of help from native-born Americans. There are only a handful of New Americans in high-level management positions—too few to offer adequate support for emerging New American leaders at stage four. That is not enough. However, we need to fully know their needs to understand the best approaches to help them.

Some people say that New Americans in stage four do not need help because they are successful already. Keep in mind the multiple challenges this group faces and the real benefits they bring to their cultural communities and to mainstream communities. These emerging leaders need help, but their needs differ. Their needs might include:

- Scholarship opportunities for those who want to continue their education or other resources to build their leadership capacity

- Flexible, open systems that help more New American leaders to move up to the mid- and high-management leadership position in business, government, and nonprofit organizations

- Support from mainstream communities and institutions to allow New Americans who work with mainstream institutions to help their own refugee communities more

- Money and support from government and corporations to help New Americans expand their businesses

- More partnership opportunities with mainstream organizations to help address refugee problems, especially those problems that go beyond the capacity of refugees

- Mainstream mentors who can help New Americans become successful leaders in their own communities and achieve their professional goals

Summary

This chapter has begun to dive into the deeper elements behind achieving success. Above all, the New American must not only succeed in the external world, but in the interior world of attitude as well. They must not only succeed in their community but in mainstream culture. They are carrying double loads, again and again. In many aspects, this fourth stage of development is beginning to look better—to look successful. Yet now is the time when a refugee leader must learn and also help his or her own people maintain a positive attitude, recharge personal energy, and draw clear boundaries about what can be accomplished in twenty-four hours. Now is not the time for mainstream culture to pull back its support or for the New American's family to relax its own support. When the New American leader learns to achieve success in two cultures while walking the extra mile, the support community must be alert to new ways to assist with continuous training and fresh resources.

Tips for Stage Four

For New Americans	For those who serve New Americans
• Develop a career plan as part of your short-term and long-term goals and strategies	• Show New Americans where to get scholarships for higher education both for themselves and for their refugee community members
• Increase your management and leadership skills and prepare to lead others	
• Build networks and support groups as a way to learn from each other	• Show New Americans how to obtain grants and access to other resources for building their cultural community
• Use your power, skills, and energy to help your refugee community	
• Do not forget to spend time with your family—balance the needs of self, work, and community	• Be a mentor or peer exchange to help New Americans gain more management and leadership capacity
• Work to keep your family together as you promised before you came to America	• Work in partnership with refugee-run organizations and funders who support programs that prepare New Americans as future leaders
• Educate the mainstream community about your cultural and community issues and ways to address them	
• Educate your refugee community about American systems and how to access resources	• Educate refugee leaders about different systems and how to access the systems—educational, business, governmental, and so forth
• Bring in resources from outside to help your refugee people	• Allow more New Americans to enter mid-management or executive positions in business, government, and nonprofit organizations
• Actively participate in the American political process to advocate for refugees	
• Be a bridge between refugee and mainstream communities	• Work in partnership with New Americans to develop or promote multicultural workplaces or programs
• Be a mentor to other refugees	• Open doors for refugee businesses to grow through tax incentives, low-interest-rate loans, or new contracts

Chapter Seven

Stage Five—Leading

L EADING—SERVING AS A MULTICULTURAL LEADER—is the highest stage of refugee development. There are only a few refugees who pass stage four and reach stage five. Here, people become multicultural leaders including business owners, government officials, and nonprofit leaders. Both refugee and mainstream communities recognize and respect these New Americans as role models and as their leaders. For the New American, this is the highest achievement of his or her career and life. They enjoy being successful people who arrived with empty hands and have become leaders for both refugee and mainstream communities in America.

Those New Americans who become elected officials take pride in being elected to lead others; at the same time they have a fear of keeping their status. They don't know what will happen to them at the next election because they usually depend on the full cross-cultural public to keep them in office—and the needs and interests of mainstream voters do not always intersect with those from the multicultural electorate. Elected officials, however, are different from business and nonprofit leaders. Business leaders enjoy their own successes of making more money and employing more people. Some may have more time to relax if they have people with the right skills working for them. For those who work with nonprofits, these leaders—like their peers—still work hard and long hours, but they are rewarded by the satisfaction of their impact on their communities.

Characteristics of Multicultural Leaders

- New Americans at this stage are happy and take pride in their successful achievements, in their financial stability, and in having the opportunity to change people's lives.
- Some become multicultural leaders for both mainstream and refugee communities, earning a high degree of respect from both communities.
- Some become champions in certain fields for both communities' interests.
- Since they are recognized as successful people, others want to learn from their successes. Therefore, many are role models and cross-cultural mentors for their peers.
- New Americans at this stage hold leadership positions in government, business, or nonprofit sectors.
- Some understand better than most how American systems work for both refugee and mainstream communities.

Those who reach stage five are usually already successful and stable individuals who are well respected and recognized within their own refugee community. They have likely been in the United States for at least twenty years, and may even be a second or third generation member of a refugee community. Only a few multicultural leaders are refugees from the first generation in America.

At this stage, New Americans (we will call them multicultural leaders) have gained full respect from both refugee and mainstream communities. They continue to help build multicultural communities by providing coaching and mentoring and sharing their experiences with other leaders. Their own cultural community, the refugee community in general, and the mainstream community recognize them and their expertise. The three communities start seeing them as cross-cultural role models who help bridge racial gaps. They design and lead some initiatives to help both refugee and larger communities. One might become a champion in a certain field such as helping the refugee business community to grow or advocating for refugees on housing, health care, or education issues.

New Americans who become multicultural leaders not only work hard but they also work smart. They are self-determining, self-disciplined, and goal-oriented people and they are also risk takers or innovators. They not only walk the extra mile; they also walk that mile in front of people to lead them. They do not just lift themselves up; they also pull others to the top with them. These multicultural leaders work hard to seek justice for all communities. They teach new lessons about diversity, cross-cultural benefits, and how to live in harmony together. They are leaders who are able to bring different community members and leaders together. They are problem solvers who know how to help communities resolve their own problems. Most importantly, they do not want to see the same mistakes repeated over and over. These leaders want to see things changed for the better.

Success Factors

New Americans who become multicultural leaders have made use of some success strategies that can inspire all of us. Many of these strategies have served them throughout life—from traveling with refugee passports to traveling with multicultural leader passports. Knowing and having resources such as money, skills, people, know-how, and good character is a big plus to helping refugees become multicultural leaders.

The roads of their journeys are long, rough, and marked by ups and downs. These strategies are:

- Favoring risk and innovation
- Working smart
- Getting the community behind them on new ventures
- Being both teacher and learner
- Good timing and choosing the right opportunities
- Cross-cultural mentoring

Favoring risk and innovation

Multicultural leaders have a higher level of risk-taking attitude than refugees in other stages, including those who are at stage four. Multicultural leaders know how to calculate their risk well and take risks without being foolish. They are not afraid of taking out loans to expand their businesses, and in so doing some then become richer. They may try introducing new things or ideas, and then later become pioneers or champions for the cause they introduced. They like to walk in front of their refugee community as they become visible leaders or elected officials.

There is the old saying that without risk, life stays at the same spot forever. Multicultural leaders plan to take risks and move on; that is the only way that they can progress. They challenge both themselves and others through their risk-taking attitudes and actions.

Risks are not new to any refugee—all refugees took risks when they escaped from one place to another to avoid fighting, imprisonment, or persecution. However, they had no choice but to flee their countries and to escape the wars for their own lives or the lives of their family. In fact, as a percentage of the total refugee population, we do not see many refugees who want to take high risks in their new lives because they are afraid of failure in this new country. From the perspective of many refugees, taking risks in the new society is uncertain or unsecured, and that is why only few New Americans pass stage four and go to stage five to become multicultural leaders.

Working smart

Working hard, seven days a week, helps some New Americans succeed in reaching their goals. But this strategy may not help them reach the top. Reaching the top requires "working smart." Different people have different ways of working smart. Working smart is more than setting priorities, balancing work and family, or setting clear expectations. But as a whole, this group of New Americans knows how to handle obstacles or resolve problems properly by getting help from the right people with the right skills at the right time. If they are employers or managers, they hire the right people to work for them. If they are entrepreneurs or leaders, they try innovative techniques to handle obstacles. They may be motivated by doing things that nobody has done before.

Others work smart by finding collaborating leaders to work on solutions and to create opportunity for their refugee community. They seek collaborators from their own refugee groups as well as the mainstream community—business leaders, educators, health professionals, police officers, funders, other social service providers serving refugees and immigrants, and elected officials. Because they know how to work smart, they see that some community issues are complex and can't be solved by a small group of refugee community leaders.

Working smart is easy to say but difficult to do. Only a few New Americans are recognized because they know how to work smart in addressing their community needs.

Getting the community behind them

Community support is a vital force that helps push New Americans to the position of being multicultural leaders. Different types of leaders need different kinds of support. For example, a multicultural political leader absolutely needs the support of his or her base refugee community, both for the real base of support that community provides and because that community's support builds legitimacy in the eyes of potential mainstream supporters. A multicultural business leader who sells products to mainstream markets or clients may not need the same type of support, but the refugee community's support and recognition still are important for other reasons: moral support, status, and the leader's sense of belonging. Often, multicultural business leaders provide financial support to the refugee-run and refugee-serving organizations within their community.

Of course, self-commitment and dedication to succeed are more important than support from community members and native-born Americans. In order of priority, multicultural leaders need family support first, community support second, and then mainstream support.

Evidence for the importance of community support comes from what happens when such support is lost. Some New American leaders make the mistake of forgetting that it's their own people who pushed them up. They may distance themselves from their refugee support community or lose touch with their own people after their personal goals of becoming multicultural leaders are met. Consequently, their own people pull back their support. With the loss of this crucial part of their base of support, they often lose the broad support they need to maintain their status at the top. Occasionally this happens with elected officials such as state representatives, school board members, and city council members. Once such support is lost, the leader can no longer legitimately play a bridging role, helping refugee and mainstream communities understand each other.

Being both teacher and learner

Multicultural leaders consider themselves both teacher and learner. They like to share their knowledge or experiences with others. They help people gain knowledge and skills through their mentoring and teaching contributions. At the same time, they learn new approaches from others. They know there is always something new to learn—about new research, about an innovative project somewhere else, and about changes in the community or neighborhood itself. Multicultural leaders value new learning experiences that help build their skills so that they are able to do effective work.

Multicultural communities are dynamic places where change is constant and it is hard to predict the outcomes. Community projects often range from working with youth to serving families, from bridging racial gaps to building leadership. Multicultural leaders love a "give-and-take" approach. They are expert on some things but not everything. Sometimes they lead and other times they follow and learn from others.

Good timing and choosing the right opportunities

It is sometimes said that if someone is at the right time and place and has the right skill and attitude, that person tends to have more opportunity to succeed with their personal and professional goals than those who do not arrive at the right time and place. There is some truth to

WORKING ACROSS CULTURES

Gadaly was an electrical engineer from Eastern Europe. He came to the United States twenty-six years ago with his wife and children. Gadaly lives in Minnesota and has worked hard for years bringing his people together through festivals, community events, sports events, and so on. He is a founder of the Slavic Community Center.

Perhaps the greatest challenge Gadaly has faced is to help Eastern European parents understand and adjust to American educational systems. At the same time, he has spent time educating American school administrators about the backgrounds and attitudes of parents from his community. In relation to youth and education, he has tried to help parents improve their relationship with their own children. He educates parents about their children's education.

Children feel that they do not have support from their parents and that their parents always push them beyond their ability to perform. The expectation of parents in his community, he says, is that their children get perfect scores. Parents tend to blame their children as stupid, lazy, or careless when they do not meet their parents' high expectations. Gadaly aims to help parents be open-minded and to learn more about American systems as he educates American administrators about the expectations of his own community. He stressed that his Eastern European parents must understand that education in Eastern Europe is different from American education systems. Parents have to understand about their Americanized children's need to achieve success for themselves rather than for their parents, as they did back home.

that. Nevertheless, opportunity never ensures success; refugees who become multicultural leaders seem to have a good instinct for seizing opportunities when they arise.

Cross-cultural mentoring

Cross-cultural mentoring has proven to be a valuable method to help refugees climb in the business and professional world. It also helps native-born Americans better understand how to work with refugees. A good mentorship relationship helps eliminate barriers, decrease mistrust between people who come from two different cultures, and increases cross-communication skills. If the personal relationship is good, a good business relationship will follow smoothly. For instance, a long-term relationship among refugees creates mutual trust, and then mutual trust leads to business success. In contrast, many Americans focus their work on achieving outcomes or taking actions rather than pursuing a process of developing their relationships. Mainstream people often perceive their business relationship as a short-term one and believe it to be terminated after certain contracts are done.

These different views of relationships shape communication and interaction with each other and their final outcomes. The closer or longer the relationship is with the refugee, the better outcomes they might have because it takes time for them to sort out the impact of their cultural viewpoints on the mentor-mentee relationship.

Communication is multidimensional and becomes even more complex when we add cultural differences. Good cross-cultural mentors are good cross-cultural communicators, and they understand how to interact with people from different cultural backgrounds. They also understand the importance of nonverbal behaviors such as how people view time, space, and silence; how people use body behaviors such as facial expressions or eye contact; and how they respond to smell or touch while they communicate. Knowing each other's cultural beliefs, practices, and values is essential for a cross-cultural mentoring program. Lack of the above elements might lead to misunderstanding and showing unintentional disrespect between mentors and mentees.

Challenges

Though they have experienced tremendous success by the standards of their own community and mainstream standards, people at stage five continue to face many challenges. The following are four common challenges:

- Breaking the glass ceiling
- Continued high expectations of their own refugee community
- Difficulty building links among refugee communities
- Balancing multiple constituencies

Breaking the glass ceiling

One of the barriers preventing refugee leaders from reaching this highest developmental stage is the concept of the "glass ceiling" and their ability to break it. The glass ceiling is a persistent barrier. It is similar to what American women have faced for a very long time—the barrier of gaining acceptance to high-paying jobs and executive positions. In addition, the multicultural leader needs to be recognized by native-born Americans as having the capacity and skills to lead both mainstream Americans and refugees. Those who are unable to break the glass ceiling do not get to challenge themselves to their highest creative potential.

Remember that most refugees have experienced some kinds of discrimination all their lives no matter what stage they are in—when in flight, in a refugee camp, and at various times in America. Much of this time refugees can't express themselves freely because they do not feel safe or secure. Even in America, many refugees do not feel secure enough to report instances of discrimination.

Breaking the glass ceiling is not simple, and it requires both a collective effort from high leadership and strong support from the refugee community, the mainstream community, and policies around refugees. Some refugee leaders feel that management systems in their workplaces do not allow them to go beyond their current position or work. Other refugee leaders feel that they are discriminated against by mainstream top managers because they are refugees and not because of their skills, expertise, or knowledge to perform their work. Many refugee leaders can see what life is like on the other side of the glass ceiling and know that it is there, but they can't pass through it. Sometimes refugee leaders know that, given the chance, they could manage or serve an executive role, but they don't have support from leadership, management, or systems to move up.

Some mainstream readers might be surprised to learn that personal and institutional discrimination against refugees is real, and our society and workplaces need to address this issue. Remember that most refugees have experienced some kinds of discrimination all their lives no matter what stage they are in—when in flight, in a refugee camp, and at various times in America. Much of this time refugees can't express themselves freely because they do not feel safe or secure. Even in America, many refugees do not feel secure enough to report instances of discrimination. Even as a refugee gains strength, confidence, citizenship, and success in America—and finally, even as a stage five person who has lived here twenty years and is a real leader—the experience of discrimination is both a historic and current part of life.

Continued high expectations of their own refugee community

The issue of high—sometimes unrealistically high—expectations within the refugee community was first addressed in stage four, but intensifies in stage five. Consider the example of a former refugee who is now an elected official. Refugee community members support or elect their leaders because they want their leaders to help them and their children lead better lives. Plus, they want to see changes or results in a short period of time. If the changes or results are not seen quickly, the refugee community can withdraw their support from their leaders.

But in elected offices, change takes months and years and it requires time, energy, resources, and people. Sometimes, multicultural leaders have all the resources in place but they still can't move projects ahead (for example, building housing for their elderly). They have to play by all the rules of American bureaucracies or politics despite the urgent demands of their refugee constituents. And, of course, as an elected official the leader represents other constituents whose demands they must also attempt to fulfill.

Meeting—or failing to meet—their refugee constituents' urgent but sometimes politically difficult needs while maintaining their support can become a barrier for the stage five leader, even if that leader is not elected. As a leader for many people, lots of needs must be balanced. And the leader is not always in the best place to help his or her constituents understand the limits on the scope of their influence.

Difficulty building links

In stage four, the leader has to deal with power struggles within a single refugee community. While these struggles continue, the new multicultural leader often has the task of bringing together multiple refugee communities—at least in regions where more than one type of refugee has settled.

While mainstream people may believe that all refugee communities have the same needs, the reality is that they differ from one community to another. For example, all refugee communities need housing. When buying houses, one community may not have a problem with paying interest, but another community may follow religious practices that forbid paying interest. The multicultural leader faced with advocating for all refugees may find that such differences create rifts among constituents.

Finding the right leader, with the right skills, at the right time is not an easy task for the refugee community. Refugees are diverse in terms of backgrounds, cultures, skills, needs, and ways of interacting. They might compete with each other because of limited resources. Individual community leaders see things differently; however, many work well together in certain areas such as capacity building or leadership development for refugees.

Balancing multiple constituencies

As mentioned in stage four, a New American's success depends on how they are able to live in two cultures (their homeland culture and American culture). In stage five, their biggest challenge is to balance their work between multiple communities—their cultural or ethnic community, their refugee community in the region, and their larger cross-cultural community (which usually includes the mainstream community).

The cultural or ethnic community is their closest community, where the refugees share their own culture—Cambodian, Hmong, Salvadoran, Somali, or Russian, for example. The refugee community in the region is the group of cultural communities from a larger named region of origin, such as the Asian community or African community. The whole refugee community represents all types of refugees in a region, for example, both African and Asian refugees within a limited geographic setting. Finally, the larger community is the new state or region in which they live. For an elected official, this is the community that votes them in and that they must represent.

If multicultural leaders spend too much of their time and energy with their cultural community in the region, the larger refugee community criticizes them. If they spend more time and energy with their refugee community in the region and leave their cultural community behind, their own cultural community criticizes them. If they spend more time with the larger community, their own cultural and refugee community in the region criticizes them. So, whatever they try to do they get criticized, and it is hard for them to balance their time, values, and efforts. In most cases, balancing their work among the three communities is impossible.

There is no magic answer for multicultural leaders. It would be wonderful if the larger community allowed their multicultural leaders to spend a little more time to help their cultural and refugee communities in the region because the two communities are far behind the mainstream. But the larger community also needs the leader's attention and representation, so multicultural leaders have to be responsible for all their constituents.

What Multicultural Leaders Need at Stage Five

The position of multicultural leader may seem one of honor and privilege, but as we have seen, the needs of such leaders are great. American society needs multicultural leaders and needs to support them. Here are some of the supports that multicultural leaders need.

- Multicultural leaders need moral and emotional support from their families and refugee and mainstream communities.
- Multicultural leaders need mainstream leaders to open systems that will support their work and allow them to take more leadership roles.

- Multicultural leaders need help from mainstream Americans to prepare them for higher levels of leadership by increasing their skills and expertise though mentoring opportunities and moral and emotional support.

- Multicultural leaders need access to financial support so they can help other refugee community leaders through mentorship or leadership programs, foster the growth of political involvement activities within their community, or otherwise nurture the next crop of leaders.

Summary

Refugees or new Americans who have become multicultural leaders have a duty to both lead and serve, to teach and to learn. Their diverse experiences and contributions are important to help build American society. American society is multicultural, and it needs help from its experienced refugee leaders.

TIPS FOR STAGE FIVE

For multicultural leaders	For those who help multicultural leaders
• Actively participate in the American political process and get involved in systems change	• Be eager to learn about ways multicultural leaders can improve America
• Increase your understanding of community needs other than those of your own specific cultural group and find common threads	• See each individual as distinct and respect him or her
• Be patient with your peers when they become multicultural leaders or assume other large leadership positions	• When mentoring or teaching multicultural leaders, make the relationship two-way—learn from the New American as he or she learns from you
• Develop new initiatives by working with different leaders to build multicultural community	• When mentoring or developing relationships, understand (and allow) that some of the information will be communicated through body language or through story, especially at the beginning of the relationship
• Bridge refugee and mainstream communities	• Envision social systems with New American leaders active in and supported by the systems
• Learn ways to "work smart" and sustain yourself for this hard work of leading in a new country	• Provide moral support for multicultural leaders and encourage them to do more to help all the communities they serve
• Help change systems to help more New Americans reach top leadership positions	• Become copartner or cosponsor for new initiatives to help the refugee community catch up with the rest of society
• Work with others to change systems that can be beneficial for both refugee and mainstream communities	• Pair with new multicultural leaders in educating the public about the refugee community's assets and contributions
• Assist in building the leadership capacity of refugee leaders through education, mentorship, or internship programs	

Chapter Eight

Advice for Refugee-Serving Organizations

THIS LAST CHAPTER PROVIDES A FRAMEWORK, tools, and tips for those who work with refugees at all stages of development and in many circumstances. It is designed for consultants, community leaders, funders, program officers, government officials, agency directors, professionals, and managers from mainstream organizations.

You have learned a lot about refugees' histories, backgrounds, unique characteristics, challenges, strengths, and developmental stages. You've learned through your personal experiences and observations and through this book. Knowing the needs of refugees before and after their resettlement in the United States is important for those preparing to assist them.

As important as it is to know about the needs of refugees, knowing their individual strengths is even more important when helping them with their resettlement.

This chapter will help you understand how to help individual refugees adjust to their new lives and develop their future goals. The developmental model you've learned about should help you get a picture for the major contributions refugees can make, as well as the difficult process they go through. Individual refugees' needs, strengths, and processes through various stages differ greatly from one person to another, even within families. These differences magnify from one community to the next. Approaches or strategies that work well with refugees from one community might not be appropriate with refugees from other communities.

In this chapter, you will have an opportunity to assess your readiness for this work. This is important because the relationship- and trust-based nature of business among refugees makes this work especially demanding of your time. You will also learn about the work itself—barriers, challenges, and the importance of relationships and trust. Finally, this chapter provides some concrete advice for institutions—government agencies, nonprofits, funders, and corporations—that wish to better serve refugee communities.

Self-Assessment

Knowing your own motivation, ability and capacity, and readiness, knowing the people you serve, and knowing how to work with them are keys to success. Please find out more about yourself by going through the assessment below. Answer the questions with regards to your feelings about refugees.

A. Your Motivation	Yes	No
Are you willing to share your knowledge and expertise?		
Are you willing to learn more about refugee individuals or groups?		
Are you willing to face new challenges (see next page)?		
Are you willing to sacrifice your time and energy?		
Are you willing to make mistakes?		
Are you comfortable working with this group of refugees?		

B. Your Ability and Capacity	Yes	No
Do you think you are the right person with the right skills and expertise?		
Does your program allow you to work with refugees?		
Do you have time and resources to help refugees?		
Do you listen well?		
Do you know the individual developmental stages well?		
Do you have any fear that you may not be able to work well with refugees?		
Do you have somebody to talk to when needed for a specific subject matter?		
C. Your Readiness	**Yes**	**No**
Are you ready to use your skills, expertise, and resources?		
Are you ready to give up power or your comfort level now and then?		
Are you ready to work with this group of refugees?		
Are you ready to start now?		

If you answered "yes" to most of the questions in Your Motivation, this means that you are mentally prepared to work with or to help refugees. If your answers tended to be "no," you should not consider working with refugees at this time.

If you answered "yes" to most of the questions in Your Ability and Capacity, this means that you have resources to help refugees such as skills, time, and connections with others who know about refugees. If you answered "no," you need to go back to your "no" answers to find ways to eliminate your barriers.

If you answered "yes" to most of the questions in Your Readiness, this means that you are the right person with right skills and ready to go. If you answered "no," you need to ask yourself if you are the right person to do this kind of work or if you should wait for a while until you are ready.

NEW TO THE FOREST

Once there was a small sleek black cat, new to this particular forest. Cat had made his way to this place among the oaks, journeying long across the tundra and swamps, and now wanted to settle here and make his life. Shortly after arriving in the first green of summer, he began to be visited early every morning by different animals in the area, all coming to help him.

The first morning there was Rabbit, soft and brown, his nose twitching curiously. He encouraged Cat to jump, and Cat could certainly jump, though not as high and far as Rabbit. He encouraged Cat to twitch his ears, and Cat could do that, too, though he could not lay his ears back as smoothly as Rabbit due to his short ears and inexperience. Rabbit hopped off into the woods.

The second morning Dog came. This was not the cat-fighting dog kind of dog, but a sweet dog who wanted to welcome Cat to the forest. Dog encouraged Cat to run fast, and Cat could do that, though not quite as fast as Dog. Then Dog barked, and encouraged Cat to bark... just like this... but of course Cat's mouth opened and a delicious, long Meooow came forth, as you'd expect. Cat could not learn to bark, yet he continued to try, and his mews became short and to the point.

The third morning, along came Bird. Like the other animals, Bird welcomed Cat to the forest, and said, "I knew your parents very well, and am glad to see you here!" Then Bird encouraged Cat to fly! Now of course, Cat was not born with wings, but he decided to try anyway. He wanted to try anything that would help him succeed in this particular forest. Cat climbed to the top of the tree and leaped out, spreading his legs wide. But no, Cat dropped quite quickly and hard onto the ground. This happened several times; Cat simply could not fly.

Finally, on the fourth morning, along swam Fish. Fish followed in the steps of all the animals before him, and encouraged Cat to be more successful, saying, "Come swim with me!" Well, now, Cat hated water and could not imagine swimming. But Fish insisted, showing how easy it was, "just move this way, ever so slightly, and turn and flip around like this." So Cat tried it, and sunk. Twice, Cat rose to the surface, splashed about, and sunk like a rock. On the third try, Cat gulped a lot of water, and sank down. It seemed that Cat was gone for good!

Suddenly Cat came sputtering up and struggled to shore. All at once he exclaimed, "I am not Rabbit! I am not Dog! I cannot bark, and I cannot fly like Bird. And, I most certainly cannot swim like Fish!"

At that point, all the animals got together into a Council of Beings and discussed what had happened. Rabbit, Dog, Bird, and Fish were quite moved at nearly losing their new friend, Cat, and felt responsible. All they had hoped to do was to help Cat be successful in the new forest. They learned a very big lesson that day, and talked in some detail about how they should do things differently.

There is a moral here for both refugees and the people who would help them. For those of you who are refugees, know your strengths. Learn, but not to the detriment of your own culture and being. For those of you working with refugees: If you don't know the refugee well, learn from him or her. Each refugee's experience is his or her own. Don't impose your own strengths on them. Learn, and help them at the same time.

Major Challenges

Three major challenges confront both refugees and non-refugees when working together. These three challenges are

- Language barriers
- Lack of cultural competency
- Lack of experience working together

Language barriers

Language barriers often prevent refugees and those who help them from understanding each other or interacting with each other. Some refugees simply have not yet learned to communicate well in English.

Mainstream people who want to help refugees also have a language problem. They likely speak one language—and that's usually not the refugee's native tongue. So both refugees and non-refugees have language difficulties that prevent them from interacting or working effectively together. Non-refugees must learn how to listen to people who speak English with different accents, especially those who come to America at older ages or those who come speaking more than one language.

Language difficulty doesn't mean that refugees and non-refugees can't work together. They can help each other through interpreters or signals. When interpreters are not available, family members, friends, volunteers, or staff from refugee-run organizations can usually help with translation.

Lack of cultural competency

Every human being is a member of one or more cultures, and these cultures influence an individual's beliefs, practices, behaviors, and personality. A person who has cultural competence has specific knowledge of other people's cultures, backgrounds, values, and beliefs as well as skill in obtaining that knowledge which he or she lacks. Further, a person with cultural competency respects and recognizes other people who have different cultures from them. This competency, then, goes far beyond knowledge to a universal sense of openness and acceptance of other human beings.

Cultural competency helps eliminate, overcome, or reduce cultural barriers when working with diverse groups of refugees and communities. Lack of cultural competency causes problems. Clumsily applying the experience gained from working with one group to another might not go well due to the differences among refugee groups. For instance, most Somalis share the same language, religion, and culture, but they are divided into groups by a deeply rooted clan structure. Because of deep clan divisions, a person who works with one group of Somalis and then tries to generalize his or her experience to apply to all Somalis can meet devastating failure.

Cultural differences between refugees and non-refugees often lead to misunderstanding or misinterpretation of messages between one person's culture and another. One's culture determines specific nonverbal behaviors or body languages, which represent specific thoughts, feelings, and meanings. Different interpretations of body language are among the most difficult problems in any cross-cultural communication.

Consider this example of how different cultures interpret messages differently though using the same symbols or gestures. In some cultures, to ask another person to come near, one moves the fingers back and forth with the palm down. In contrast, in the United States one moves fingers toward the body with the palm up. This may not seem to be a big deal, but in some cultures, calling someone with the palm up is the way to call animals, inferiors, or slaves. What an insult! Without intending—and likely unknown to the person who uses the signal—this simple hand signal can turn off an entire group of people. Therefore, culture plays an important role in our nonverbal communication and other interactions with one another.

In some ways, cultural competence comes down to getting to know, in depth and as friends, the people you work with. Try the following:

• Involve refugees in your projects and learn how they approach or interact with their own people

- Make friends with refugees and learn more about them and their cultural practices
- Learn about different cultures by taking classes or workshops or by doing your own research
- Invite guest speakers to talk about how to improve your work with a specific community
- Have personal contacts with refugee communities you serve or attend community cultural events such as New Year celebrations
- Volunteer at local agencies by tutoring English, teaching citizenship classes, or becoming a board member
- Develop peer networks with refugees and invite them to teach you about their own cultures and business practices
- Have (or hire) staff from relevant refugee communities in order to provide cultural and linguistic services appropriate to those refugee communities

TIPS FOR WORKING WITH OTHER CULTURES

If you are not a member of a cultural or ethnic group with which you work, be aware of the following:

- Do not touch anywhere in someone's head area. For most cultures, the head is considered the most sacred part of the body, where the brain is and thinking processes take place.
- Do not use your feet to point to an object, kick to get attention, or touch someone with your foot. For some cultures, touching someone with your foot is considered very disrespectful to that person.
- Do not use a finger with your palm up when you call someone because that person might think that you view him or her as a slave, inferior, or animal.
- Do not joke about any family members, especially women if you do not know them well.
- Designate a place of worship for those who need to pray during their break time.
- Respect apparel that is culturally important to the group.

Lack of experience working together

Lack of (or limited) experience working together is one of the major challenges faced by both refugees and non-refugees. Problems range from different communication styles to different work approaches, from lack of patience to personality clashes, or from lack of time to lack of trust.

Previous experience working with one particular group of refugees is a plus—but not sufficient. Therefore, learning more about specific groups of refugees is a key strategy for your success when working with refugees.

While there are many categories of difference from one group to another, four elements have an impact on how refugees and non-refugees work together. These require conscious attention as the relationship is developed.

- Appropriate protocol among people with authority
- Different concepts of time
- Preferred forms of communication
- Lack of patience

Appropriate protocol among people with authority

Different cultures have differing approaches to authority—and typically, when an outsider approaches a refugee group to provide assistance, that person automatically has "authority." He or she must also know the rules for how authority is granted and how authorities treat each other within the culture. Further, these rules are usually unspoken and may be expressed through nonverbal cues.

Consider this true story: A consultant I know was contracted by a foundation to assist an Asian organization. He and the executive director of the Asian organization agreed that he would meet with all the board members at a board meeting. The main purpose of that first meeting was to find out the scope of a financial issue faced by the organization related to misuse of funding. The consultant waited outside the boardroom for hours for his turn on the agenda. The executive director came and checked with the consultant every thirty minutes with several excuses about why the board wasn't ready for him yet—the board had a lot of things to discuss, they were sorry to keep him waiting, etc., etc.... After three hours of waiting, the consultant talked to the executive director to reschedule their meeting because he could not wait longer. Later, the consultant learned that there was an entirely different set of messages being communicated.

The executive director did not want the consultant to talk to his board members directly due to a need for saving face and maintaining his reputation.

The executive director could not say "no" to the consultant when the consultant proposed to meet with his board due to his culture. In other words, it was culturally inappropriate for the consultant to have asked the executive director to meet with the board, but also culturally inappropriate for the executive director to tell the "expert" consultant "no."

The consultant did not know how to read the nonverbal cues of his client. His client, nonverbally, had cued him that the meeting was inappropriate when he first asked to have it. Further, each time the executive director came out of the meeting to tell the consultant "they were not ready," he really meant "please go." Though both consultant and executive communicated in English, they were truly speaking different languages.

Needless to say, there were a great many failures in this first contact. An already touchy financial situation—difficult for any consultant in a standard relationship—was exacerbated by the consultant's failure to understand the rules of the culture he was entering and to understand the cues of the client.

Different concepts of time

Time concepts vary widely from one culture to the next. Mainstream Americans who do not have experience with refugees often grow impatient with what they perceive as wasted time. Here, mainstream people need to understand the different approaches to time. But refugees also ought to learn and change their attitudes, behaviors, and practices when using their time with mainstream people. In the mainstream culture, being on time shows their respect for others. Mainstream Americans are often time-bound. Schedules and lists dominate their own lives, and everything they do must be on time including catching trains, planes, and meals between everything. Mainstream people tend to perceive time as a linear movement. In contrast, people from many parts of the world see that activities and relationships—not clocks and calendars—determine their actions and priorities. They perceive time as a circular movement, and they believe that time will come back tomorrow, next season, or next year.

Non-refugees should not generalize that every group of refugees is the same and that all refugees come to meetings late. Some groups of refugees or individuals are on time and respect time the way the mainstream population does. Remember, each individual and each group is different—get to know them and adjust your work process accordingly.

Preferred forms of communication

In my own experience working with refugee groups, effective ways to communicate with refugees are not by letter, voice mail, e-mail, or other written forms. Here are preferences of methods to communicate with others:

1. Meeting face-to-face is the most preferred method for most refugee groups
2. Communicating through the phone, but not leaving a message, is their second preference
3. Communicating through e-mail and following up with voice mail, is their third preference

The three preferred methods above might not be applied to the younger generation of refugees because they are more Americanized and more direct when they communicate with others. Remember that individual refugees have different styles and approaches when they communicate. This might come from their cultural influence and experiences they have from their own country or from personal preference.

Lack of patience

It is almost impossible for non-refugees to work effectively with refugees without showing patience, especially when working with those who have not had formal education or have little experience working with Westerners or Americans. Patience, commitment, and persistence are necessary for those who work with refugees in all communities. Things we have planned are not always achieved the way we want when working with refugees. For example

- Meeting times with refugees can be changed very often during planning and implementation processes. As a person planning to work with refugee groups, you might not expect or accept (and hence plan for) the delay. Remember, most refugee groups have extended families and whole communities demanding their time.

- Response time from refugees may seem to be too slow. Remember, they might want to check with family or community members about an important decision.

- Misunderstandings often occur due to communication barriers, cultural differences, or lack of experiences working together. It's better to plan for such occurrences than be taken by surprise.

Learning about Differences

Refugees bring with them their own cultures, values, beliefs, and worldviews—which may or may not overlap with those of mainstream Americans. When developing work (and personal) relationships, both refugees and non-refugees need to make a conscious effort to identify differences in their cultural, familial, communication, and work styles. Knowing these differences helps both refugees and non-refugees avoid making mistakes. The cultural continuum/checklist on the next page can be used to identify your preferences.

← ——————————— **CULTURAL CONTINUUM** ——————————— →

Self-orientation __	__ Collective orientation
Direct communicator __	__ Indirect communicator
Talker/Verbalizer __	__ Thinker/Listener
Short-term relationships __	__ Long-term relationships
Nuclear family focus __	__ Extended family focus
Linear movement of time __	__ Circular movement of time
Mastery over nature __	__ Harmony with nature
Action-oriented __	__ People-oriented
Materialistic __	__ Spiritual
Competitive __	__ Cooperative/non-confrontational
Self-promoting __	__ Self-effacing (modest)

After finding your own place on the continua above, you need to find the general place that represents the refugees you work with. Work to learn how your cultural values shape your choices. Learn more about the cultures, backgrounds, and communication styles of the refugees you work with by trying the following tips:

• Pay close attention to inner group membership, relationship, authority, role, power, and social status. Sometimes a person who is at the table does not have decision-making power or cannot make a decision for himself or herself.

• Expect refugees to ask you about your age, income, and social status, which may be against your cultural norms. In some cultures, people want to know the above because they respect people with older age or higher social status.

• Spend more time to get to know and foster your relationship with refugees and learn more about them. The more time you spend in the beginning to build relationships and trust, the less time you will spend at the implementation phase.

• Look for nonverbal cues such as facial expression, voice expression, body language, or gestures. Adopt a listening and learning role for a while. Ask about the person's experiences and preferences and ask for feedback on your communication.

- Listen to long introductory stories with two ears—one to the facts of the story and one to the message buried within the story. Some cultures are more likely to communicate complex ideas through a story rather than in a "direct" mode.

- Find ways to shift the relationship you have with refugees from a hierarchical one, as perceived by refugees, to one of equal partners. Some ways to do this include recognizing their contributions and strengths and offering your emotional or technical support for their work.

- Help refugees save face by avoiding confrontation or public criticism. If necessary, the criticism should be done in private rather than in public.

- Pay attention to the word "yes" because, sometimes, refugees cannot say "no" when their friends or bosses ask them to do something. For some refugees, saying "no" to their friends or bosses is rude or impolite. Check this out with them if you have any doubt about their nonverbal cues.

- Try to understand the cultural values regarding close or reciprocal relationships among the groups with which you are working. Some groups of refugees might value the relationship over the work if they have to help their friends.

- Expect that refugees may behave very formally when they first meet you. In some cases, their behavior might seem overly polite or unfriendly to you, and you might not like it. In some cases, this is how they show their respect; in others, it is due to them seeing you as an outsider. In either case, you will need to take time to build trust.

- Be cautious in your use of the Western merit-based reward system that singles out individuals, rather than the group, for superior performance. Most refugees come from collectivist societies, with an emphasis on teamwork and equal distribution of rewards. A reward to one individual would need to be given to the group, with the credit shared and equally distributed among all. (Since not all refugees come from collectivist cultures, don't assume that the merit system should not be used. Just be sure to check out which system will be most appreciated and have the desired effect within the culture.)

- Try to understand more about how reciprocal relationships work in the culture with which you are interacting. For some groups, giving a gift to someone who helps them is an important way to show that they are a respectful person; this is not bribery but a demonstration of good manners.

- Don't assume that people you are working with will make the leaps and conclusions you expect them to when you are communicating with them. Take the time needed to lay out all your facts and to connect one idea to its conclusion, and that conclusion to the next conclusion, and so forth, until your position is clear.

- Allow refugees time for religious practices and plan meetings accordingly. Similarly, do not serve foods that are contrary to the religion. For example, when working with groups who practice Islam, meeting times may need to include time for prayer and foods with pork violate their traditions.

- Learn more about different interpretations of nonverbal behaviors with those you serve or will serve.

Appendix B contains information on communication styles and can help you better understand some of the cultural factors that influence communication. Just remember that with all of these assessments of cultural and communication style, you are dealing with generalizations. Nothing can replace your personal knowledge of your own approach and your honest attempts to respect and understand each individual you encounter.

Relationship and Trust Are Keys to Success

Relationship and trust are essential for success when working with refugees. Skills and knowledge are necessary but not sufficient. Having good relationships and trust makes work easier, faster, and more effective.

The role of relationships

As described in Chapter 7, personal relationships normally have priority over business relationships for many refugee communities. Personal and public relationships frequently overlap or mix, and it is hard to separate them from each other. Long-term relationships play a very important role in facilitating or easing the work with refugee individuals, their families, and their communities.

Here's a simple example of how good, long-term relationships with refugees ease work. I was asked by my manager to conduct an interview with six Asian executive directors for one of her projects with another refugee group. My manager told me that she had called and left them messages for almost two weeks, and not a single director had called her back. She was under pressure to provide a final report to her clients. I started calling those six executive directors, whom I considered as close friends, to set up the interviews. Within three days, I had scheduled and completed all the interviews. These executive directors were busy with their work, but they gave me their time because they had an obligation to help their friends when needed, and they knew I would do the same thing for them. They had not scheduled time with my manager because they lacked the personal relationship—and sense of interlocking obligations—that I had.

Building trust

Culture and past experiences influence matters of trust among refugees. In general, refugees are more likely to trust people only after they have demonstrated their trustworthiness, while mainstream people tend to trust people until there is reason to withhold their trust. Past experiences and culture both influence this; refugees do not naturally trust outsiders beyond their own families or community members. As a result, they do not say what they mean and they do not do what they say. Especially at the beginning of relationships, non-refugees have to pay close attention to building trust when working with refugees. After trust is ensured, some refugees are open, honest, and straightforward, and tend to share almost everything with others without hiding their personal secrets, problems, thoughts, or stories. They will say what they mean, and they will do what they say. Fostering relationships and building trust with refugees takes time and commitment. Work with them will be faster and easier after the relationship and trust are built. However, when relationships and trust are damaged, everything you have built with refugees is lost, and sometimes it is hard or impossible for you to rebuild trust.

Where does distrust come from? Broken promises, dishonesty, inconsistency, self-promoting behavior, or unethical behavior all generate distrust. If you or your organization has lost trust among refugee groups, regaining it takes time and effort. There are a number of ways to build and regain trust with refugees. Please check the following:

- Treat refugees fairly and with respect—the way they want to be treated
- Learn more about their cultures, customs, values, and cultural practices
- Demonstrate your consistency between word and deed by avoiding all hidden agendas, hidden interests, or secretiveness
- Show your motivation or willingness to work with refugees, and do not expect them to always come to you
- Keep your promises—say what you mean and do what you say— and inform refugees if changes are taking place
- Do not harm or discredit refugees for your own personal gain
- Accept your own mistakes by showing your willingness to correct them
- Set aside time for face-to-face meetings with refugees periodically to find out if anything is going wrong between you and them
- Answer questions honestly

Partnering Roles for Government, Nonprofits, Foundations, and Corporations

Much of this chapter has been aimed at practices for the individual who wants to work with refugees. Yet often refugee work is either fostered by or directly involves government agencies, nonprofit organizations, foundations, and businesses. Each of these can play significant, different roles. Following are three ways that these groups can work together to improve situations for refugees in America: build collaborations and partnerships; use long-term strategies; and address specific needs of specific communities. After that are some actions each type of organization can take.

Build collaborations and partnerships

We cannot reach our common goal of serving refugees or refugee communities without strong and effective collaborations or partnerships among nonprofits, foundations, public and private institutions, refugee communities, and citizens. These groups must work together when providing services to refugee communities. Some issues faced by refugees—such as youth development, adapting to the education system, availability of health services, and lack of affordable housing—cannot be solved by refugee communities, nonprofit organizations, or government agencies alone. The government needs refugees and nonprofit organizations to carry out specific jobs because they know the issues in the communities better; the nonprofits also need government and foundation funding and support. In short, we all need each other to do this well.

Collaborations and partnerships among various refugee-assisting groups are key. These should be broadened to include other institutions such as small businesses, corporations, job agencies, faith-based groups, community development corporations, and diverse cultural and ethnic groups. Typical refugee problems such as unemployment, housing, and child care are very complicated and require public and nonprofit entities to work together.

TRUST BACKWARD!

I'd like to share a simple model called "trust backward" that I developed to use when starting work with a new group of refugees and with refugee individuals. I call this model Trust Backward because its initials are TSURT—TRUST backwards. The end result of this model is to help you build closer relationships and create more trust.

T Try to learn about and get to know individuals or a group of refugees more—their backgrounds, developmental stages, problems, needs, and assets or strengths. AND, **try** to change your behavior when you make a mistake or when you do something that's not appropriate for the culture.

S Seek similarities or experiences you have in common with different groups of refugee people. For example, your ancestors came from Europe as immigrants or you have a friend who is a refugee; while part of the mainstream culture, you come from a group that is historically oppressed; your background, like the particular refugee's background, emphasizes closely knit extended families; while your foods are different, both your culture and the refugee's culture use large, ritual feasts as a part of social bonding.

U Understand refugee individuals better—especially their cultural values and beliefs, norms, experiences, thinking processes, and nonverbal communication behaviors such as personal space, time concepts, silence, relationships, etc.

R Relationship-building is essential to improve communications and work more effectively between mainstream and refugee individuals. Learn the role of relationships in work and personal life for the culture you are interacting with—and follow them. In some cultures, one develops a warm personal relationship first; a good public relationship will follow.

T Trust-building is a key to success when working with refugee people. Refugees tend to distrust a stranger or outside groups—both because of traumatic, past experiences and, in some cases, because their culture influences matters of trust in others. Most refugees are more likely to trust people only after those people have shown they are trustworthy.

Use long-term strategies

Remember, it can take twenty years for some refugees to become full participants in American society. Therefore, institutions serving refugees should set long-term strategies to help build the capacity of refugee individuals, communities, and organizations. It takes time for these individuals and groups to "catch up" with the rest of American society. They need appropriate tools, knowledge of community development, and an understanding of American systems. Only then will they be able to provide better services to their own people and build better communities.

Effective long-term strategies can include supporting the refugees' own self-help systems and organizations that assist their own people in meeting basic needs. Similarly, agencies can participate in and support efforts to bring different refugee groups together to share their common goals and create long-term strategies to address the needs of their communities. Successful initiatives must be created in order to draw on funding, expertise, experience, and influence from outside resources to help refugees.

Address specific needs of a specific community

On the large scale, it is clear that most refugees will face language, employment, and cultural adjustment barriers. They'll need appropriate English and job skills in order to get better jobs to support their families. But in attempts to help, agencies will miss the boat if they use a "one-size-fits-all" approach to serving refugee communities.

Providers and practitioners must understand the specific needs of the specific communities they serve. For example, some groups of refugees are focusing on survival and resettlement—finding adequate housing, coping with cultural adjustment, overcoming loss and isolation, and learning English. They find local jobs as parking lot attendants, cab drivers, or factory workers. They also face major challenges of social and cultural adjustment. Women who are accustomed to staying home and being supported by their husbands must now go to work to survive. Men who are accustomed to having two or three wives are now allowed to have only one.

After almost twenty years of assimilation into American culture, some refugee groups still struggle to balance the demands of a strong cultural heritage and the challenge of being new Americans at home, work, and in school. In the past, their family lives were practiced under their own clan system. Clan leaders are from the older generation while more professionals are usually from the younger generation.

Do you see that a single family adjustment program can't be designed for all refugee groups? For example, the needs of refugees from the Mideast will differ dramatically from the needs of Central Americans. The needs of Hmong refugees will differ from those of Somalis. The agency that wants to help must clearly understand the backgrounds, cultures, needs, and assets of specific refugee communities and individuals. These agencies must develop programs that rely on the widely diverse abilities and gifts of the differing populations to envision and build their own futures and to solve their own problems.

Furthermore, the whole of American society will become stronger and more powerful as it learns to integrate many cultures. Elements of many cultures, when added into American ways of doing things, will make us all wiser, more adaptable, and more resilient.

Guidelines for Various Agencies

The advice above fits all types of entities—government agencies, mainstream nonprofits, refugee-run organizations, foundations, and corporations. Yet each of these has some specific tasks they can undertake to help make the system function better for refugees.

Government agencies

- Educate refugees about American systems and where refugees can find available resources
- Allocate special grants for refugee students—to help fund higher education for both refugee adults and youth

- Educate Americans about refugees' and especially new arrivals' histories, backgrounds, needs, and contributions
- Help other government agencies at all levels better understand refugee communities and groups, especially new communities they serve
- Provide financial support to help refugees beyond the first two stages of life in America
- Be patient

Mainstream nonprofits

- Understand the histories and backgrounds of refugees and develop programs to fit their changing needs
- Redirect programs that help refugee youth achieve their higher education
- Develop programs that do not strongly compete with refugee-run organizations, especially meeting the current needs of refugees
- Work with refugee-run organizations to build their leadership capacity so they are able to provide better services to their own people
- Work with others to advocate for refugees in changing systems to better fit the needs of refugees
- Help refugee organizations or individuals better understand American systems and business operations
- Serve as facilitators or interpreters who help refugees understand and gain access to systems and resources
- Be patient

Refugee-run organizations

- Educate your refugee community about American culture and cultural norms, appropriate behaviors in the workplace, educational systems, and political process
- Educate your refugee community about two main priorities—improving English skills and getting a higher education—to which refugees must devote their time and energy
- Support each other's work through collaboration

- Help government, foundations, and mainstream institutions better understand how to help refugees
- Work with mainstream nonprofits to advocate for systems change in order to open the systems that can be responsive to help refugees
- Increase your partnership and collaboration with your refugee groups by using your mass power to reach more people
- Educate others about specific needs and culturally appropriate behaviors when working with specific groups of refugees

Foundations

- Continue to provide funds for specific programs—but don't limit those (as is often the case) to education for youth who finish high school, housing for elderly, or individuals who want to pursue their higher education
- Designate funds for employment programs that help refugees move up from assembly workers to supervisory positions
- Hold educational forums that focus on helping refugees move out of stage two faster by promoting programs that increase the capacity of refugees
- Promote programs that help refugees get involved in systems change or in the political process
- Designate funds to support study or research about a refugee community's programs and their successful models
- Commit to funding for the long-term; refugee adjustment takes decades

Corporations

- Assign refugees to sit on diversity committees or community relations committees
- Allow refugees to meet with other refugee groups, discuss their concerns, and then present their concerns to higher management for actions to improve the corporation

- Get refugees involved in new product development or ask them for feedback to improve products
- Provide internship opportunities so refugee employees can prepare themselves for higher positions
- Avoid all stereotyping when hiring, firing, or promoting individuals; model new and flexible human resource systems and internal policies

Summary

Working with refugee communities is time consuming—but deeply rewarding. In this work, you will have the opportunity to build deep, long-lasting friendships that are not the norm in other American work relationships. You will learn much about your own culture and personality as you get to know the cultures, histories, and styles of the groups and individuals you hope to work with. Knowing these differences can save costly mistakes when working with refugee populations. And, at a deeper level, knowledge of these differences will also cause you to want to know more. Relationships are key, as always, but especially when working with refugees because of their past experiences. If you work slowly to a build a deep level of trust, you will benefit greatly. The goal is a better life experience for all who come to America's shores, and this goal is best met when we all learn and work together. Finally, never underestimate the benefit to America when its refugees are welcomed, heard, learned from, and woven into the tapestry of society. This is one path to a stronger America.

Appendices

Appendix A

Selected Publications, Web Sites, and Organizations

PUBLICATIONS

Immigrant and Refugee-Led Organizations and their Technical Assistance Needs

MOSAICA: The Center for Nonprofit Development and Pluralism.
1522 K Street, NW, Suite 1130,
Washington, DC 20005
202-887-0620
http://mosaica.coure-tech.com/resources/ford.pdf

This report of a study conducted for the Ford Foundation summarizes and analyzes technical assistance needs and experiences; describes current and possible models for technical assistance to immigrant- and refugee-led organizations.

Rising with the Tide, Capacity Building Strategies for Small, Emerging Immigrant Organizations

LA Immigrant Funders' Collaborative
PO Box 1100
Sebastopol, CA 95473
213-559-8304

This publication provides grantmakers and technical assistance providers with knowledge and tools to build the capacity of immigrant and refugee organizations in Los Angeles County and across the country. This report is available by contacting Grantmakers Concerned with Immigrants and Refugees.

Equal Justice, Unequal Access: Immigrants and America's Legal System, Recommendations for Action and Collaboration

Asian American Justice Center (formerly the National Asian Pacific American Legal Consortium)
1140 Connecticut Avenue, NW, Suite 1200,
Washington, DC 20036
202-296-2300
www.advancingequality.org/files/equaljustice.pdf

One of the largest organizations in the country focused on providing multilingual, culturally sensitive legal services, education, and civil rights support to Asians and Pacific Islanders. This report details the barriers immigrants face when trying to access the American legal system and provides recommendations on how these barriers can be minimized or eliminated.

WEB SITES

Forced Migration Web Site
www.forcedmigration.org

A worldwide site that offers lots of information about refugees and immigrants, from refugee laws to health issues of forced migration people including children and elderly. It links you to other resources— journals and databases; academic research institutes; governmental, inter-governmental, and multilateral institutions; non-governmental agencies; and non-electronic resources and a bibliography.

International Thesaurus of Refugee Terminology
www.refugeethesaurus.org

Provides an online service for users to select specific terms from an alphabetical display of terms or to locate specific terms such as "refugee" and "asylum seeker."

U.S. Citizenship and Immigration Services
www.uscis.gov

A U.S. government web site that provides information for refugees and immigrants who resettle in the United States, including how to apply for green card and for U.S. citizenship. It provides legal forms, benefits, laws, regulations, and guides.

ORGANIZATIONS

African Services Committee in New York City
429 West 127th Street
New York, NY 10027
212-222-3882
www.africanservices.org

A community-based organization in New York City dedicated to improving the health and self-sufficiency of the African community. It provides direct health, housing, social, and legal services to over 10,000 African refugees, asylum seekers, and immigrants each year with an emphasis on HIV/AIDS prevention, treatment, and support. It employs over thirty staff from more than fourteen African countries.

Canadian Council for Refugees
6839 A Rue Drolet #302
Montreal, QC H2S 2T1
514-277-7223
www.web.ca/~ccr

A nonprofit umbrella organization committed to the rights and protection of refugees in Canada and around the world and to the resettlement of refugees and immigrants in Canada.

The Center for Victims of Torture
717 East River Road
Minneapolis, MN 55455
612-436-4800
www.cvt.org/main.php

The Minnesota-based Center for Victims of Torture (CVT) is a private, nonprofit, nonpartisan organization founded in 1985. The first organization of its kind in the United States and the third in the world, CVT has pioneered a comprehensive assessment and care program that is unique in the United States. Its "Resource Manual for Teachers" provides teachers with an excellent tool when teaching refugee youth.

Centre for Refugee Studies, York University
Room 321, York Lanes
4700 Keele Street
Toronto, ON M3J 1P3
416-736-5663
www.yorku.ca/crs/

This research and educational institution provides both undergraduate and graduate programs for those who want to become an expert on refugee affairs.

**Cross-Cultural Counseling Center
of the International Institute of New Jersey**
880 Bergen Avenue
Jersey City, NJ 07306
201-653-3888
www.iinj.org

Provides a range of services designed to help newcomers, their families, and communities become self-sufficient, contributing members of American society. It also provides confidential mental health services to the Haitian, African, Russian, Vietnamese, Chinese, and other Asian communities.

Ethiopian Community Development Council
901 South Highland Street
Arlington, VA 22204
www.ecdcinternational.org

*The Council serves as a welcoming presence and a bridge for dia-
logue and education. Through its programs, ECDC seeks to empower
African newcomers by giving them hope for their future and helping them quickly become self-sufficient, productive members of their
communities in their new homeland.*

The Florence Immigrant and Refugee Rights Project
PO Box 654
Florence, AZ 85232
520-868-0191
www.firrp.org

*Provides free legal services and advice to men, women, and children
detained by the Bureau of Immigration and Customs Enforcement
(ICE).*

Hmong Cultural Center
995 University Avenue W, Suite 214
St. Paul, MN 55104
651-917-9937
www.hmongcenter.org

*This center and its web site provides information on Hmong studies,
culture, arts, books, organizations, religious groups, and media in
the United States.*

Immigrant and Refugee Community Organization (IRCO)
10301 NE Glisan Street
Portland, OR, 97220
503-234-1541
www.irco.org

*One of the largest refugee- and immigrant-led organizations in the
United States. Provides refugees, immigrants, and multi-ethnic communities with variety of services such as the Asian Family Center, the*

International Language Bank, youth and family services, employment programs, community education, health and environmental outreach services, and arts for new immigrants program.

International Organization for Migration (IOM)
17, Route des Morillons
CH-1211 Geneva 19
Switzerland
+41/22/717 9111
www.iom.int

The IOM web site provides publications, research studies, and reports about migrant people in Asia, Central America, Africa, and Eastern Europe.

International Rescue Committee
122 East 42nd Street
New York, NY 10168
212-551-3000
www.theirc.org

In the United States, the IRC helps new arrivals get settled and adjust and acquire the skills necessary to become self-sufficient.

Lutheran Immigration and Refugee Service
700 Light Street
Baltimore, MD 21230
410-230-2700
www.lirs.org

One of the nation's leading agencies in welcoming and advocating for refugees and migrants. Its web site links to organizations serving refugees locally, nationally, and internationally.

New Iowan Centers
Iowa Workforce Development
150 Des Moines Street
Des Moines, IA 50309
515-242-6240
www.iowaworkforce.org/centers/newiowan/index.html

A community "one-stop-shop" for anyone new to Iowa. Coordinates services to immigrants with relocation needs and questions.

Administration for Children and Families (ACF)
U.S. Department of Health and Human Services
370 L'Enfant Promenade, SW
Washington, DC 20447
www.acf.hhs.gov

A federal agency funding state, territory, local, and tribal organizations to provide family assistance (welfare), child support, child care, Head Start, child welfare, and other programs relating to children and families.

Refugee Council USA
3211 4th Street, NE
Washington, DC 20017
202-541-5402
www.refugeecouncilusa.org

The Refugee Council USA provides focused advocacy on issues affecting the protection and rights of refugees, asylum seekers, displaced persons, victims of trafficking, and victims of torture in the United States and across the world. Their web site provides annual refugee admissions figures, NGO statements related to refugees, and consultation documents on refugees.

The Refugee Studies Center
Queen Elizabeth House
University of Oxford
Mansfield Road
Oxford OX1 3TB
United Kingdom
+44 (1865) 270722
www.rsc.ox.ac.uk

This center conducts research and teaches courses and consequences of forced migration, including a series of psychological training modules.

Refugee Services of Texas
200 East 8th Street
Austin, TX 78701
512-472-9472
www.rst-austin.org

Helps refugees in the Austin, Texas, area with their resettlement through services of reception, replacement, social/health, employment, and language.

Southeast Asia Resource Action Center
1628 16th Street, NW, 3rd Floor
Washington, DC 20009
202-667-4690
www.searac.org

Offers leadership development for nonprofit organizations led by Southeast Asians (SEA), advocates for SEA communities, conducts action-oriented research, and provides an online directory of SEA organizations in the United States and other publications about Southeast Asians.

UNITED for Intercultural Action
Postbus 413
NL-1000 AK Amsterdam
Netherlands
+31-20-6834778
www.united.non-profit.nl

A European network against nationalism, racism, and fascism and in support of migrations and refugees.

United Nations High Commissioner for Refugees (UNHCR)
www.unhcr.ch

Provides basic information about refugees and updates current refugee movements around the world. Readers can find different sources of publications and statistics about refugees.

USA for UNHCR
1775 K Street, NW, Suite 290
Washington, DC 20006
202-296-1115 or 800-770-1100
www.unrefugees.org

Provides educational resources about refugees through games, videos, posters, annual reports, and updates on refugee issues.

U.S. Committee for Refugees and Immigrants
1717 Massachusetts Avenue, NW, 2nd Floor
Washington, DC 20036
202-347-3507
www.refugeesusa.org

Readers can find refugee reports from 1979 to present and summaries of regional and individual countries that produce and assist refugees in Africa, East Asia and the Pacific, South and Central Asia, the Middle East, Europe, and the Americas.

Appendix B

Cross-Cultural Communication and Conflict

—By Marion Peters Angelica, PhD

T HIS SECTION IS ADAPTED from pages 25–33 of *Resolving Conflict in Nonprofit Organizations: The Leader's Guide to Finding Constructive Solutions* by Marion Peters Angelica.[15] In this section, Angelica provides a background to cross-cultural communications, with some advice on how miscommunications across culture can result in conflict. It is adapted here as a general guide to the influence of culture on communications, and to help you understand the relationship between communication and conflict.

Not only are we products of individual temperament, unique life experience, family upbringing, and established mental patterns, we are also products of the culture in which we live or have lived. Culture establishes many of our communication patterns as well as our basic values—and often, these are so familiar that they are invisible to us. When not understood, these cultural patterns can be a source of conflict. An understanding of cultural differences can be the key to conflict resolution, however. This book offers a brief overview of cultural patterns as a way to alert you to things to consider when you confront a conflict.

Note: The descriptions of culture here are generalizations used for example. Don't assume that a person from a particular background shares these general views.

The role of culture in conflict

In general, people raised in non-Western cultures perceive and deal with conflict differently from people of Western European backgrounds—and there are plenty of unique characteristics even among different Western European people. Two key elements shape the way people from different cultures deal with conflict. First is a culture's shared beliefs and values about harmony and conflict. Second is the culture's communication style, both in language and gesture. These two elements are best understood within a broader framework that anthropologists use to view different cultures.

Geert Hofstede, a noted Dutch anthropologist, classifies contemporary societies on a continuum with two end points—collectivist cultures and individualistic cultures. In collectivist cultures, activities and decisions are geared to preserving and enhancing the cultural group. In individualistic cultures, activities and decisions are geared to preserving and enhancing the individual. Most cultures display a mix of collectivist and individualistic characteristics. These characteristics influence how people deal with conflict when it arises, and some may actually give rise to conflicts when people from collectivist and individualistic cultures interact. (See Figure 4.)

Hofstede based his approach on the work of Edward Hall. Hall, a scholar viewed as a major force in the study of intercultural communication, developed the concepts of high context and low context cultures and was the first to clarify some of the major communication differences between them.[16]

High context communication

According to Hall, in high context communication the message contains relatively little information. The people exchanging messages already hold most of the information, which they learn during the continuing acculturation process throughout their lives. They need and

---

[16] Adapted from G. Hofstede, *Cultures and Organizations: Software of the Mind* (New York: McGraw-Hill, 1991), 67, 73. Adaptation by Marion Angelica, *Resolving Conflict in Nonprofit Organizations: The Leader's Guide to Finding Constructive Solutions* (Saint Paul, MN: Fieldstone Alliance, 1999), 26.

FIGURE 4. KEY DIFFERENCES BETWEEN COLLECTIVIST AND INDIVIDUALISTIC CULTURES[17]

Collectivist Cultures	Individualistic Cultures
People are born into extended families which protect them throughout life in exchange for loyalty	People are born into an immediate (nuclear) family that offers protection largely through childhood
Identity is based on the social network to which one belongs	Identity is based on the individual and his or her ideas and accomplishments
Children learn to think in terms of "we"	Children learn to think in terms of "I"
Harmony is valued and should be maintained; direct confrontation should be avoided	Individual expression is more valuable than harmony; direct confrontation is acceptable
Trespassing norms leads to shame and loss of face for the individual and the group	Trespassing norms leads to guilt and loss of self-respect
Employer-employee relationship is perceived in moral terms, similar to a family link	Employer-employee relationships is perceived in contractual/legal terms based on the notion of mutual advantage
Hiring and promotion decisions take the employee's social networks into account	Hiring and promotion decisions are based on individuals' skills and rules and disregard social networks
Management is management of groups	Management is management of individuals
Relationships are more important than tasks	Tasks are more important than relationships
Collective interests prevail over individual interests	Individual interests prevail over collective interests
Private life is open to the group; privacy is not a right	Private life is not open to the group; privacy is a right
Opinions are predetermined by group membership	Opinions are expected to be developed by the individual
Laws and rights differ according to the group to which one belongs	Laws and rights apply equally to all
Harmony and consensus in society are ultimate goals	Self-actualization by every individual is ultimate goal
Communication is high context (see definition on page 164)	Communication is low context (see definition on page 166)

[17] Edward Hall. *Beyond Culture* (Garden City, NY: Doubleday Anchor Books, 1976).

desire only the unique and specific information particular to the instance about which they are communicating. Japanese, Arab, and Mediterranean people, with their extensive information networks among friends, family, and colleagues, are high context communicators.

These cultures contain many communally accepted concepts, principles, and practices. Expecting to receive only unique and specific information from messages, people may view the inclusion of communally known information as patronizing or wasteful. For example, in a job interview in Japan, the job seeker will be specifically asked about family and friends during the interview—the unique information expected from the communication. He or she will not be asked about skills, knowledge, or abilities because these are known, based on the reputation and status of the university the job applicant attended. In Japan, there is a known hierarchy of the quality and rigor of the education offered at different universities. The placement of the university in this hierarchy conveys information about skills, knowledge, and ability. Both university graduates and corporate employers know which university's graduates match the needs of corporations. Consequently, hiring decisions at Japanese corporations are primarily based on the applicant's networks—family and friends—the unique information about the individual. (Given these hiring practices, many new immigrants from Asia and the Middle East find standard hiring practices in United States organizations quite baffling.)

Low context communication

In low context communication cultures, relatively little communal information exists among the people communicating and much information is contained in the message itself. People in such cultures expect lots of information and data. Americans, Canadians, and northern Europeans tend to be low context communicators. For example, in a low context culture like the United States, it is expected that considerable background data and potential consequences will be presented to decision makers before a decision is made. Not providing this information, even if decision makers already know some or all of it, is viewed as careless or suspect (as though someone is withholding necessary information). Offering this level of information in a high context culture would be viewed as presumptuous, disrespectful, and a waste of people's time.

American, Canadian, and northern European cultures have the characteristics of individualistic cultures. Most South American and Asian cultures have the characteristics of collectivist cultures. When people from these cultures work together, it is important to understand different expectations about communications.

Here is an example of a conflict that arose specifically because of cultural differences. A large Midwestern nonprofit employing over three hundred people hired a qualified individual who had been raised and educated in Central America. Her job was to facilitate the organization's communications with local Spanish-speaking communities. One of her tasks was to set up and document several community forums to get input from Latino community members about issues on which the organization worked. After six months, the employee and her supervisor discussed how the job was going. The employee was shocked to learn that her supervisor was unhappy with her performance: She had organized only one forum and had yet to write it up. Also a number of the employee's colleagues had complained that she continually interrupted them to ask them to review and revise her written communications. They complained that they were doing her work as well as their own.

The supervisor thought the employee showed poor time management skills and a lack of task orientation. From the employee's perspective, she had made excellent use of her time. She had gotten herself appointed to three task forces in different Latino communities and had made many contacts over the past six months. She was also astonished at her peers' reactions to her requests that they review her written materials. Her understanding was that this is what professional colleagues do for one another.

Through lengthy discussion, the supervisor and the new employee learned how their cultures influenced their perspectives on the job. The supervisor and the other employees were task oriented, while the new employee was relationship oriented. What peers had viewed as interruptions and avoiding work, the new employee saw as important workplace relationship building and professional interaction. The behavior of all involved stemmed from their cultural perspectives about how to effectively get work done. Together, the supervisor and new employee decided how best to connect the organization with the Latino communities while respecting their different cultural contexts.

The role of communication style in conflict

The second general element that influences conflict is communication, both verbal and nonverbal. While individuals from the same culture often have different personal communication styles, they still share many culturally specific patterns of communications. A shared language is one. Even so, misunderstandings about the meaning of words are still a big source of conflict, even among people who share the same language.

Though our choice of words can sometimes avert or create conflict, language is only one means by which we communicate. Experts estimate that 60 to 90 percent of communication occurs through vehicles other than words. Intonation, smiling, laughter, pace, gesture, posture, eye contact, and physical distance all have culturally specific meanings. A gesture or expression that one culture views as positive, another will view as negative. Needless to say, it is easy to misinterpret nonverbal communication, particularly if we assume that other people's nonverbal communication has the same meaning as ours.

In regard to nonverbal communication, we are like the fish that doesn't know it swims in water until it jumps out. It is not until we try to communicate with people from different cultures that we learn about the nonverbal communication medium in which we've been swimming. Nonverbal communication is learned early in life, mostly by imitation and assimilation. Therefore we are largely unconscious of it. Our unconscious gestures and postures only become evident when they are not understood or are misunderstood.

As an example, consider how different people use their eyes when communicating. Americans of European heritage often look up and to the corner of their eyes when trying to recall information. This same gesture indicates disbelief in several other cultures. Can you imagine how confusing this might be in a meeting between two people who understood these gestures differently? One person thinks they are conveying thoughtfulness, while the other person reads the gesture to mean disbelief. Most people are not even aware that they make certain gestures, let alone that they convey different meanings. This makes clearing up misunderstandings based on unconscious gestures a real challenge.

Anthropologists who specialize in nonverbal communication estimate that the face alone is capable of creating 250,000 expressions. There are 5,000 distinct hand gestures possible. In all, the human body can produce about 700,000 different nonverbal signs.[18] Some say that many of these signs are much stronger than punctuation in writing or intonation in speech.

Following is a brief introduction to nonverbal communication—just enough to alert you to these cultural waters. In the United States, where people of many backgrounds live and work together, individuals frequently combine elements from their cultural heritage with elements from the mainstream culture. As a consequence many people's nonverbal communication styles are based, in part, on how long they and their families have lived in the United States. This is further confounded by the strength of a person's identification with their cultural heritage. In other words, don't generalize from what follows; instead use it as a guide to learn more about the individuals with whom you associate. With this important caveat in mind, some generalities follow.

Space

North American people tend to stand about thirty inches apart (one arm's length) in normal conversation. In Asia, people generally stand farther apart, except for Chinese people, who generally stand closer than arm's length. Standing closer than the culturally comfortable distance can be understood as either aggression or intimacy depending on the situation. Standing farther than the culturally comfortable distance can convey disinterest.

[18] R. Axtell. *Gestures: Do's and Taboos of Body Language Around the World* (New York: John Wiley & Sons, 1991), 10–11.

Touch

North American people, along with many northern Europeans and the Japanese, are often not comfortable with touch among non-family members. Cultures for whom touch is much more casual and comfortable are those of most of the Middle East, Russia, Italy, Greece, Spain, Portugal, and most of Latin America. Greetings that include hugs or kisses, along with touching (generally between the same sex) during conversation, are standard ways to convey connection in touch-oriented cultures. The same actions can cause discomfort and negative reactions in cultures that are not touch oriented.

Handshakes

Handshakes are recognized as a standard means of greeting in business throughout the world, even when bowing and other forms of greeting are standard in the culture. However, how people shake hands can carry unintended meanings. North Americans of European heritage value a firm handshake, which they interpret as sincere and forthright. American Indians, Middle Eastern people, and Asians prefer gentle handshakes, which convey peacefulness and nonaggression to them. To cultures that use a gentle handshake, a firm one can be misunderstood as aggression; to cultures that use a firm handshake, a gentle one can be interpreted as a lack of commitment or interest. In many cultures, handshakes across gender are not acceptable.

Silence

North Americans are known for their discomfort with silence in conversation. Silence in a number of cultures—American Indian, Japanese, and Chinese, for example—is perfectly acceptable and viewed as showing reflection and respect. In these cultures, filling silences unnecessarily is considered rude.

A Japanese friend of mine, a professor of American culture, accompanied me to a faculty meeting at the university where I teach. He noted many differences between the ways in which faculty meetings are conducted in Japan and the United States, but an especially notable difference was the lack of silence in our meetings. At this meeting, as soon as the head of the department finished speaking, faculty members had many comments and questions. My friend explained to me that in Japan there would have been a long silence after the director spoke to demonstrate that the faculty were respectfully considering what had been said. Then, if my friend, a junior level professor, had questions or comments he would wait silently until all the professors who were his seniors had spoken.

Eye contact

Eye contact is expected and understood to indicate interest and forthrightness among European Americans, Eastern and Northern Europeans, and Saudi Arabians. However, in American Indian cultures, many Asian cultures, the West Indies, and Puerto Rico, the avoidance of direct and prolonged eye contact is a sign of respect. Similarly, some African Americans may avoid eye contact as a sign of respect. Misinterpretation of preference for eye contact can lead to serious misunderstandings between people of different cultures.

Smiling and laughter

Smiling and laughter not only indicate pleasure or happiness but also surprise, embarrassment, anger, confusion, apology, or even sadness. In several Southeast Asian cultures and in Indonesia it is considered impolite to disagree with someone in public. Smiling and laughter can indicate the discomfort that comes with disagreement. In Korea, Japan, and Taiwan laughing with an open mouth is considered rude, so laughing is usually done behind a hand.

Gestures with hands, arms, and feet

Gestures made with hands, arms, and feet convey innumerable meanings. Here, however, are some of the meanings of common gestures:

- Arms akimbo (hands on hips) can be read as a very defiant posture in Latin American and Indonesia
- Hands in the pockets are impolite in France, Belgium, Japan, and Sweden
- Pointing fingers is considered impolite by American Indian, English, Chinese, and Japanese people
- Showing the sole of the foot or shoe is highly offensive in many cultures of the Far and Middle East

Appendix C

Summary of the Stages

The tables on the following pages summarize the key information from each stage of refugee development.

SUMMARY OF STAGE ONE—ARRIVING

Characteristics

- Refugees arrive physically at their final destination
- Feelings of relief and joy
- The dream of a safer place to live comes true
- Some feel that they are "reborn"
- They celebrate one of the most important achievements in their lives
- Some miss their homeland and family members
- Some refugees receive great amounts of help from others (family, friends, sponsors, community members, resettlement groups)
- Some feel that everything around them is new and good
- They start learning how to behave to avoid mistakes
- They face essential, short-term needs, and other long-term needs after six months, for both material and emotional support

Challenges

- Difficulty communicating and interacting with others
- Finding basic necessities such as food, clothing, and shelter
- Lack of transportation or fear of traveling alone
- Trouble adapting to the new environment and culture
- Dealing with overwhelming issues

Tips for new arrivals	Tips for those who help new arrivals
• Celebrate and enjoy a great achievement in your life	• Allow new arrivals to celebrate and enjoy their new lives
• Be open to learning new things by observing and listening to others	• Provide new arrivals with simple instructions and show them basic life skills such as using a stove and electricity
• Be positive about your new life and feel comfortable about new things around you	• Do not bombard new arrivals with too much information at once
• Ask questions first before doing things you don't know, such as how to use a stove or electricity	• Be supportive by providing translation or transportation
• Ask your sponsors or family where you can get help when needed	• Take them to meet other community members and friends
• Learn the value of a dollar, how to use currency, and how to go shopping	• Bring new arrivals to the welfare office and help them apply for public assistance
• Learning English is your first priority and will help you look for a job to support your family	• Bring them to have a physical check-up at a public health department or a hospital
• Apply for public assistance	• Bring their kids to have immunization shots before starting school
• Look for an affordable home	• Help parents enroll their children in school
• Have someone teach you how to use public transportation	• Help them find affordable housing
• Ask your sponsors or family members how to enroll your children in schools	• Take them with you when shopping or going to the grocery store

SUMMARY OF STAGE TWO—ADJUSTING

Characteristics	Challenges
• Refugees confront numerous difficulties in their adjustment phase	• Language and cultural barriers
• Refugees face many barriers, including language and culture	• Culture shock
• Refugees have a hard time eliminating their old, painful memories and grieve over the loss of or separation from family members	• Lack of transportation
• Adjustment problems become more complex and more difficult for outsiders to understand	• Stark geographic change
• Refugees face countless new life experiences	• Change in traditional roles
• Some children start off or fall behind in school due to language barriers and lack previous formal education	• Intergenerational conflicts
• Elders are isolated and lonely at home, and some have poor health	• Barriers to employment
• Some families cannot find housing	• Concerns about the future of new generations
• Refugees are frustrated and depressed; some lose their sense of self, their self-esteem, sense of competence, and so forth	• Racism and discrimination
	• Health problems

Tips for refugees	Tips for those who help refugees
• Think positively about your new lives here	• Try to understand refugees' problems through their story telling and nonverbal behaviors
• The new challenges you face are only temporary, and you are not alone when you face them. Support each other as much as possible	• Provide refugees with advice, support, and assistance in dealing with everyday life and American ways of life
• Have physical checkups regularly and follow the doctor's recommendations	• Help refugees better understand and trust the banking system—to use banks rather than hiding money
• Talk to sponsors, family members, and friends about your problems	• Remind them to take care of themselves—going to see doctors, allowing time for exercise, and eating the right foods
• Seek professional help if you think that your feelings (your emotional state) are not normal or you feel depressed	• Help the elderly deal with social isolation and depression
• Get a driver's license as soon as possible and save money to buy a car	• Refer refugees to available resources for themselves and their family members
• Attending English as a second language (ESL) classes to improve your communication and English skills	• Provide transportation assistance or help getting their driver's licenses
• Look for a job. Consider that public assistance is temporary, and you must become self-sufficient as soon as possible	• Help them to enroll in English as a second language (ESL) classes
• Focus on school because education is key to your future success and for your children's success	• Help refugees with their resume, understanding the interview process, or applying for their first job
• If you are a parent, learn new parenting skills to help children deal with two different cultures	• Volunteer to help children improve their school performance through tutoring or after school programs
• Comply with all immigration laws and requirements	• Help parents with translation at school conferences
• Make contact with others to explore your future opportunities	• Teach refugees about American culture or how to interact with Americans
• Make friends with Americans and learn more from them about how they interact with others or about their culture	

SUMMARY OF STAGE THREE—CLIMBING

Characteristics

- Refugees create their own personal, future plan based on their hopes and dreams
- Refugees upgrade job skills
- Some get better jobs with good benefits
- Some earn college and technical degrees
- Refugees understand American cultural norms better
- They know and adapt to American ways of life
- Refugees can communicate in English with others more comfortably
- They show comfort with surrounding environments
- Some refugees save money to buy a new home or open small businesses
- Children improve school performance and completion rates
- Some refugees attend citizenship classes
- Refugees understand local banking and school systems better

Challenges

- Continued language barriers
- Lack of a clear career plan
- Lack of a life balance
- Lack of support system
- Lack of financial and academic supports
- Family troubles in the homeland

Tips for refugees	Tips for those who help refugees
• Take care of yourself and make sure that you stay healthy	• Remind refugees to take care themselves or to slow down if you see that they need to relax
• Learn to balance needs of self, family, and work	• Try to understand the refugees' strengths and assets when you help them
• Develop educational goals—get your higher education and look for scholarship opportunities	• Provide refugees with clear guidance and options in developing their new career plans
• Upgrade your skills— job skills, communication skills, and social skills	• Help them improve their communication skills, especially written and oral language skills
• Look for new jobs that support your future goals	• Provide them with resource information so that they are able to access different resources
• Get out of public assistance and stand on your own two feet	• Support refugees when they are new to their job or when they are stuck in low-paying work
• Plan your lifelong journey and implement it with patience and care	• Refer refugees to the right people with the right skills when they need help
• Use all your strengths, assets, and support systems to achieve your goals	• Educate refugees about American systems and appropriate ways of doing business in the United States
• Do not let bad situations back in your homeland drag you down, ruin your future, or make you feel hopeless	• Help them get their citizenship
• Get your citizenship, if time permits	• Provide them with resources so they can get licensure and certificates faster
• Get involved with your refugee community and learn more from others	
• Provide moral support to other refugees and let them support you too	

SUMMARY OF STAGE FOUR—ACHIEVING

Characteristics	Challenges
• Refugees or New Americans have the ability and know-how to do the same things that native-born Americans can do	• Difficulties in applying knowledge and skills
• Some become mentors, and help their own refugee people reach their dream goals	• Balancing personal and family issues
	• Dealing with high expectations from their own refugee community
• Some become administrators or managers in nonprofit, government, and private business	• Wrestling over power
• Some hold leadership and mid-management positions	• Keeping family together as they promised to each other before coming to America
• Some play bridging roles between their own and mainstream communities	• High expectation of their own ethnic community on leader
• Some have their own small businesses and hire their own people to work for them	• Staying with two cultures—own and dominant
• Some gain more respect from their own and other refugee communities	• Overcoming communication barrier
	• Maintaining current status
• Some are active in building refugee communities	• Competing with people who were born here for high position job
• Some become resource people for their own community or organization	• No energy or resources to help own refugee community
• Most understand American systems	• Difficulties in applying knowledge and skills learned in own community

Tips for New Americans	Tips for those who serve New Americans
• Develop a career plan as part of your short-term and long-term goals and strategies	• Show New Americans where to get scholarships for their higher education both for themselves and for their refugee community members
• Increase your management and leadership skills and prepare to lead others	
• Build networks and support groups as a way to learn from each other	• Show New Americans how to obtain grants and access other resources for building their cultural community
• Use your power, skills, and energy to help your refugee community	• Be a mentor or peer exchange to help New Americans gain more management and leadership capacity
• Do not forget to spend time with your family—balance the needs of self, work, and community	• Work in partnership with refugee-run organizations and funders who support programs that prepare New Americans as future leaders
• Educate the mainstream community about your cultural and community issues and ways to address them	
• Educate your refugee community about American systems and how to access resources	• Educate refugee leaders about different systems and how to access the systems—educational, business, government, and so forth
• Bring in resources from outside to help your refugee people	• Allow more New Americans to enter mid-management or executive positions in business, government, and nonprofit organizations
• Actively participate in the American political process to advocate for refugees	
• Be a bridge between refugee and mainstream communities	• Work in partnership with New Americans to develop or promote multicultural workplaces or programs
• Be a mentor to other refugees	• Open doors for refugee businesses to grow through tax incentives, low-interest-rate loans, or new contracts

SUMMARY OF STAGE FIVE—LEADING

Characteristics

- New Americans are happy and take pride in their successful achievements, in their financial stability, and in having the opportunity to change people's lives
- Some become multicultural leaders for both mainstream and refugee communities
- Some become champions of certain fields for both communities' interests
- Since they are recognized as successful people, others want to learn from their success. Therefore, many are role models and cross-cultural mentors for their peers
- New Americans at this stage hold leadership positions in government, business, or nonprofit sectors
- New Americans understand how American systems work for both refugee and mainstream communities

Challenges

- Breaking the glass ceiling
- Continued high expectations of their own refugee community
- Difficulty building links among refugee communities
- Balancing multiple constituencies

Tips for multicultural leaders	Tips for those who help multicultural leaders
• Actively participate in the American political process and get involved in systems change	• Be eager to learn about ways multicultural leaders can improve America
• Increase your understanding of community needs other than those of your own specific cultural group and find common threads	• See each individual as distinct and respect him or her
• Be patient with your peers when they become multicultural leaders or assume other large leadership positions	• When mentoring or teaching multicultural leaders, make the relationship two-way—learn from the New American as he or she learns from you
• Develop new initiatives by working with different leaders to build multicultural community	• When mentoring or developing relationships, understand (and allow) that some of the information will come in through body language or through story, especially at the beginning of the relationship
• Bridge refugee and mainstream communities	
• Learn ways to "work smart" and sustain yourself for this hard work of leading in a new country	• Envision social systems with New American leaders active in and supported by the systems
• Help change systems to help more New Americans reach top leadership positions	• Provide moral support for multicultural leaders and encourage them to do more to help all the communities they serve
• Work with others to change systems that can be beneficial for both refugee and mainstream communities	• Become copartner or cosponsor for new initiatives to help the refugee community catch up with the rest of society
• Assist in building the leadership capacity of refugee leaders through education, mentorship, or internship programs	• Pair with new multicultural leaders in educating the public about the refugee community's assets and contributions

Index

More books available from Fieldstone Alliance

Collaboration Handbook
Creating, Sustaining, and Enjoying the Journey
Michael Winer and Karen Ray

Shows you how to get a collaboration going, set goals, determine everyone's roles, create an action plan, and evaluate the results. Includes a case study of one collaboration from start to finish, helpful tips on how to avoid pitfalls, and worksheets to keep everyone on track.

192 pages, softcover, Item # 069032

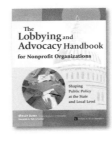

The Lobbying and Advocacy Handbook for Nonprofit Organizations
Shaping Public Policy at the State and Local Level
Marcia Avner

The Lobbying and Advocacy Handbook is a planning guide and resource for nonprofit organizations that want to influence issues that matter to them. This book will help you decide whether to lobby and then put plans in place to make it work.

240 pages, softcover, Item # 069261

The Community Leadership Handbook
Framing Ideas, Building Relationships, and Mobilizing Resources
James R. Krile

Based on the best of Blandin Foundation's 20-year experience in developing community leaders, this book gives community members the tools to bring people together to make change.

280 pages, softcover, Item # 069547

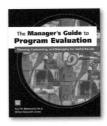

The Manager's Guide to Program Evaluation:
Planning, Contracting, and Managing for Useful Results
Paul W. Mattessich, Ph.D.

Explains how to plan and manage an evaluation that will help identify your organization's successes, share information with key audiences, and improve services.

96 pages, softcover, Item # 069385

A Fieldstone Nonprofit Guide to Forming Alliances
Linda Hoskins and Emil Angelica

Helps you understand the wide range of ways that they can work with others—focusing on alliances that work at a lower level of intensity. It shows how to plan and start an alliance that fits a nonprofit's circumstances and needs.

112 pages, softcover, Item # 069466

Resolving Conflict in Nonprofit Organizations
The Leader's Guide to Finding Constructive Solutions
Marion Peters Angelica

Helps you identify conflict, decide whether to intervene, uncover and deal with the true issues, and design and conduct a conflict resolution process.

192 pages, softcover, Item # 069164

Visit **www.FieldstoneAlliance.org** to learn more about these and many other books on community building, nonprofit management, funder capacity, and violence prevention. You can also sign up to receive our free "Tools You Can Use" e-newsletter. Or, call 1-800-274-6024 for a free catalog.

1-800-274-6024 | www.FieldstoneAlliance.org